HER BILLIONAIRE BOSS

An Overnight Billionaire Bachelor Romance

By Laura Ann

This is a work of fiction. Similarities to real people, places, or events are entirely coincidental.

HER BILLIONAIRE BOSS

First edition. May 8, 2019.

Written by Laura Ann.

DEDICATION

To the redhead who refused to give up on me,
And continues to teach me about true Christlike love.
Your friendship is one of my greatest treasures.

ACKNOWLEDGEMENTS

No author works alone. Thank you Victorine,
You and your sister make it Christmas every time
I get a new cover. And thank you to my Beta Team.
Truly, your help with my stories is immeasurable.

PROLOGUE

"I can't decide if we're desperate idiots, or desperate geniuses," Eli Truman grunted as he swung his sledgehammer into the stone wall.

"Does it really matter?" Nelson, his youngest brother said with a laugh. "Either way, we're still here, covered in dust, dirt and who knows what else, renovating an ancient castle." His eyes darted toward the shaking ceiling. "That's going to come down on us at any moment if you don't ease up with the wall toppling."

Eli grunted again, but rested the sledgehammer at his feet.

"You two are the idiots. Everyone knows I'm the brains of this operation," Hayden, the middle brother, said as he hefted an armful of lumber into the space they were working in.

Avangarde castle had become the brothers' last hope. Eli was fresh off a divorce, Hayden had recently gotten fired from his chef job in New York and Nelson had joined the venture because he held no commitment elsewhere. Together, they had pooled their resources and purchased the crumbling structure of bricks they now stood in. The plan was to bring a section of it it up to code and open a bed-and-breakfast.

Nelson rolled his eyes. "Knowing how to make whipped cream doesn't make you a genius."

Hayden glared. "No, but knowing the difference between faux gras and pate might."

"Give it a rest, guys," Eli, ever the diplomat, said as he hefted the sledgehammer again. "After I get this wall down, we can see what we have to work with."

With a loud grunt, he swung one last time. Dust rained from the ceiling and all three men ducked and covered their heads.

Once they had stopped coughing, Nelson spoke. "Geez, Eli. Got anger much?"

Eli wiped sweat and dirt from his forehead. "Sorry. That stupid stone has been here for hundreds of years. It doesn't exactly want to come down."

Hayden cocked his head as he stared with narrowed eyes at the wall. "Dude, we might be in more trouble than we thought. It looks like you broke the wall."

"That was the whole point, *Genius*," Nelson sneered as he walked over to examine Eli's progress.

"Not that wall." Hayden dropped his lumber and made his way across the messy work site. "This one." He put his hand out and pushed against what appeared to be a depression in the stone. "Whoa." Hayden's eyes widened, and he stepped back quickly, nearly tripping at the sight of the wall shifting inward to reveal a hidden opening.

"Dude! Seriously?" Nelson bounded across the room and stuck his head in the small door. "That's awesome!"

"What is it?" Eli asked as he carefully made his way over.

"Dunno," Nelson grinned over his shoulder. "But we should find out."

Hayden scowled. "Are you serious? There's probably rotting bodies or something in there." He folded his arms across his broad chest. "No, thank you."

Nelson rolled his eyes again. "Rotting bodies? No one has lived here for like a hundred years, any bodies would be complete dust by now, Genius."

"Stop calling me that," Hayden growled.

Nelson's eyebrows shot up. "You're the one who claimed you were so smart, just following your lead... Genius."

Hayden leaned in nose to nose with his little brother. "Don't make me get my carving knives."

Nelson gave a fake shiver. "Ooh, now I'm scared. A guy who spends his time in an apron and puffy hat is gonna hurt me."

Hayden reached out and grabbed Nelson, putting him in a head-lock before he could react.

With a laugh and holler, Nelson grabbed Hayden's wrist and twist-ed his way out, using his years of martial arts training to evade further attempts of imprisonment.

"CHILDREN!" Eli shouted, grabbing them both by the shoulders. "Knock if off for a minute, huh?" His face went back to the hidden door. "I think we should figure out what's going on here." He nodded his chin toward the hole. "If there are hidden rooms, they'll affect the structural integrity of the building and we need to know what we're dealing with."

"True enough," Hayden said, rolling his neck and swinging his arms as if he were warming up for a sports contest.

"Maybe you should stay here, Bro. We wouldn't want to have an accident and hurt your whisking arm or anything," Nelson said with a smirk,

Hayden glared and stepped forward, but Eli stopped him with a hand to his chest. "Where are the flashlights?"

Nelson hurried into the other room and was back in a few seconds. "Here we go! One for each of us. Sorry, Hay, I couldn't find your pretty princess one. It must still be packed in your luggage upstairs." He laughed. "Ouch!" He rubbed the back of his head when Eli slapped him.

"Knock it off, Squirt. One of these days I won't stop him from pounding you into the ground."

"Like a guy who went to school to wear a skirt could pound me," Nelson muttered while rubbing his head.

Eli turned his flashlight on and pushed the door open as far as it would go. The door was thick and after the first couple of inches, didn't move easily. The squeal of the hinges made it clear that it hadn't been opened in many years.

With a deep breath, Eli stepped into the darkness. "Oh, man." He coughed a couple of times and swiped in front of his face. "Dang, the dust and cobwebs are thick."

"This is going to be epic," Nelson whispered. "How many dead people do you think we'll find?"

Hayden shook his head. "You're such an idiot."

"And you're such a girl!"

"Shut up," Eli growled. "Nelson, go grab that broom." He put his hand on his hip and flashed his light around. "Maybe I can use it to clear the cobwebs so we can actually walk in there."

"Coming right up, Boss." Nelson worked his way through the construction zone and grabbed a beat-up broom that was sitting in the corner.

"Thanks," Eli murmured as he studied the passageway. He looked over his shoulder. "Here we go." Setting his jaw, he held the broom in front of him, swinging it slowly from side to side as he worked his way inside. "There's a staircase in here!" Eli called, surprise evident in his tone.

"Where does it go?" Nelson called back.

Hayden scowled. "How the heck is Eli supposed to know?" He shook his head. "Idiot," he mumbled.

"I meant for him to find out... why are you always so grumpy? You catch more flies with honey than vinegar, Dude. You, of all people, should know the difference between the two."

Hayden scowled and stepped into the space after Eli.

"Careful, these steps are pretty narrow." Eli's voice echoed slightly as it came up the stone walkway.

"Got it," Nelson yelled, leaning over Hayden's shoulder to answer.

Hayden flinched and covered the offended ear. Grumbling something under his breath, he stepped further into the darkness.

Slowly, the three brothers made their way down the dark and musty stairwell. The air felt heavy with moisture, and an aura of tension settled on each brother as they continued down the seemingly never-ending steps.

"This place is creepy." Nelson said as he glanced behind him at the darkness. "Oof!" Just as he turned back around he ran into something solid. "Dude! Why did you stop?" Nelson rubbed his chin where he had smacked into Hayden's head.

"Watch where you're going and you won't have that problem," Hayden muttered. "Eli stopped, so I stopped."

"There's a door," Eli called from the front.

All three brothers focused their flashlight beams to the front. A solid wood door, tall and straight, stood before them.

"Is it locked?" Hayden asked, his normally taciturn voice had lightened to awe.

Eli put his hand out and rested it on the dusty knob. Flexing his muscles, he twisted hard and the heavy door opened slightly. A puff of cold air hit the brothers in the face.

"Whoa..." Nelson breathed.

Eli glanced over his shoulder, his eyebrows furrowed together, before taking a deep breath and shouldering his way into the room.

"Eli? You still alive?" Nelson called out after a few moments of silence.

Hayden elbowed his baby brother in the chest. "Can you shut up for once?"

"What?" Nelson rubbed his chest. "It's a legitimate question."

Hayden looked at the ceiling and shook his head. "Come on," he growled. Slowly, they walked into the dark room.

Eli had stopped only a few feet inside the doorway, still as a statue.

"What's going on?" Hayden slapped a hand on Eli's shoulder.

Eli's jaw was slack and his eyes focused into the darkness. Without saying a word, he pointed a finger in front of him. Nelson and Hayden followed his finger and focused their flashlights the same direction as their older brother.

Hayden's eyes widened and Nelson gasped.

"Dude, are you all seeing this?" Nelson's voice was quiet and shaky.

Both of his brothers nodded, but didn't speak.

"I don't think we're desperate anymore," Eli finally mumbled.

CHAPTER 1

"Well, Mrs..."

"It's Miss. Miss Monson," the woman sitting across from Eli interrupted.

"Sorry, Miss Monson. As I was saying, everything appears to be in order." Eli's face was emotionless as he shuffled the papers in front of him before looking up at the middle-aged women in front of him. "We will be contacting people later in the week to let them know the results of our hiring." He stood and the woman eagerly jumped to her feet, fluffing her hair. Eli held out a hand. "Thank you for coming in, we'll be in touch."

"You're welcome." Miss Monson smiled as she gripped his hand and fluttered her eyes a little. "I mean, thank you for your time." She giggled and shrugged her shoulders.

"Yes, well," Eli's long legs took him over to the door of his brand new office and he quickly opened it. "Have a nice day."

"You too." She watched him as she walked past, wiggling her fingers in goodbye as she slowly moved out into the hall.

Eli shut the door firmly behind her. "You've got to be kidding me," he moaned as he slumped into his desk chair. The smooth, buttery leather of the seat didn't so much as squeak as he settled in. "Money might not buy you happiness, but at least it buys comfortable chairs," Eli mumbled as he lay his head back and closed his eyes.

"How goes the job hunt?" Hayden asked as he stormed into the office.

"Probably about as well as yours." Eli peeked through one eye. "Have you filled all your spots in the kitchen?"

9

Hayden huffed and fell back on the sofa on the far wall. "Half the people coming in to interview are women looking for a date, not a job." He ran his fingers through his hair.

Eli held in another groan. Last year, the three Truman brothers had become instant billionaires, not to mention media sensations, when they had discovered a room full of hidden treasure in the old castle they were struggling to renovate. Low on funds and down on their luck, they had plans to redo only enough of the castle to rent out a few rooms and open a bed-and-breakfast.

When they had literally struck gold, they had jumped at the opportunity to turn the old castle into a resort destination with each brother overseeing a specific part. Eli worked in hospitality, Hayden was a chef and had built an in-house restaurant and Nelson had created an outdoor program that utilized the several hundred acres that had come with the castle. They had even made plans to move their twin sisters to the resort once they were graduated and help them find a place to work.

Now, a year after their discovery, the resort was set to open, but the brothers were struggling to find good candidates to fill all the positions necessary to make it run. Hundreds of resumes had come flooding in, but the vast majority were from single ladies wanting to get a glimpse of what the media had dubbed 'The Overnight Billionaire Bachelors'.

Eli smirked. "How many of them left in tears?"

Hayden scowled. "I haven't made anyone cry today."

"Yet," Eli mumbled.

"Shut up." Hayden growled, then quirked an eyebrow. "Have you filled all your spots?"

Eli groaned. "No, I'm running into the same problem you are. The last one in here had to have been at least fifty, if she was a day, and she giggled at me. Actually giggled!"

Hayden chuckled. "I don't think I got that one in the kitchen. She must only be after the oldest brother."

Eli threw his stress ball at Hayden, who caught it with a laugh. "Anyway, I still have a couple more interviews today."

"What position are they for?" Hayden tossed the ball in the air and caught it.

"Front desk clerk," Eli replied after looking at the paperwork. "It shouldn't be that hard to find a friendly person who can answer phones and make reservations. It's not rocket science."

Hayden smirked before throwing the ball back. "Good luck with that," he said as he stood and headed to leave.

"Oh!" A feminine voice gasped when Hayden suddenly threw open the door.

Eli's head snapped up at the sound; a slight shiver running down his back. *What the heck is that?*

"Sorry," Hayden said gruffly.

"No, no. It was my fault. I shouldn't have been standing so close. I was just about to knock, because, I mean..." The voice sighed. "Sorry, I ramble when I'm nervous. I have an appointment with Mr. Truman."

Hayden folded his arms and smirked. "Which one? Technically, there are three of us."

"Oh, right," the voice gave a light laugh that resembled the tinkling of a bell. "Sorry. I'm looking for Mr. Eli Truman."

Without conscience thought, Eli jumped to his feet and hurried toward the doorway. "I'm Eli Truman," he stated louder than necessary, coming up behind Hayden. *Whoa...*

A petite, redheaded beauty stood in the hallway. Light from the large windows in the foyer was playing around her head, giving her porcelain skin an otherworldly glow. But it wasn't her skin that drew Eli's attention. It was the set of full, pink lips that were shaping a perfect 'O' that caught and held his stare. *Holy-*

When he managed to drag his eyes from her lips up to her eyes, he nearly choked. Wide, emerald eyes, almost too wide for her petite features, stared back at him.

"H-hi," she stuttered out. "I have an appointment."

"He's ready for you," Hayden said, turning to slap Eli on the back.

The whack woke Eli from his trance. "Uh, yes. Of course. Come in, please." He schooled his features into the stoic facade he always put on for the public. *Beautiful or not, this is just a job interview.*

"Good luck, Brother," Hayden said with a chuckle.

Eli scowled at him, but Hayden closed the door before he could see it.

"So, you are..." Eli forced himself to walk calmly around to his desk and look at his schedule. "Miss Thompson?"

"Yes, Ivy Thompson," she said softly, still standing awkwardly by the door.

"Have a seat, please," Eli waved his hand toward one of the chairs sitting close to his desk.

"Thank you," Ms. Thompson murmured and followed his directions. She sat down, primly folding her hands in her lap.

"I have here that you are looking for a position at the front desk?" Eli glanced up at her.

"Yes, sir."

"You can call me Mr. Truman," Eli stated.

"Yes, Mr. Truman, sir."

Eli glanced up and noticed a small smile on her face. It slowly melted when he didn't smile back. "So, tell me Miss Thompson, why you are looking to work at Avangarde Castle?"

"Well," her eyes dropped to her lap, "I'm looking to make a change and recently moved to this side of the state." She looked up and tried to smile at him again.

Eli watched her in fascination. Her whole countenance was sweet and airy and seemed to shine a light on the dark parts of him that had shut down after his divorce.

"I was planning to start looking for work soon and saw this pop up in the paper. It seemed ideal." She gave a light shrug.

"Do you have any experience in hospitality?" Eli kept his eyes firmly on the paper in front of him. *Being attractive doesn't make her qualified.*

"No. But I've worked in retail, so I'm pretty good at handling people and solving problems."

Eli grunted. "You understand that working at the front desk would mean handling multiple things at once? You have to be able to answer phones, take reservations and solve issues that might arise from those staying at the hotel?"

"Yes, Mr. Truman." There was no teasing in her tone anymore.

Good. She knows I mean business.

"Just how old are you, Miss Thompson?" Eli blurted out before he thought better of it.

Her eyes widened, and she stiffened in her chair.

Eli closed his eyes. *Now you've done it. You're not allowed to ask those kinds of questions.* "I apologize, Miss Thompson. It's just that you look too young to-."

The petite woman in front of him sniffed and crossed her legs. "Being small makes me look younger than I am. And yes, I know you're not supposed to ask me that, but just to ease your mind, I'm twenty-five."

Too young for you, Eli. Better steer clear of this one. He shook his head. *What the heck? I'm steering clear of all of them! No more women for me, thank you very much.* "Good to know," Eli said curtly. "Thank you for your time, Miss Thompson, we will be contacting people at the end of the week, after we have finished all the interviews."

"All right, thank you for your time, Mr. Truman." Miss Thompson stood and stepped forward with her hand outstretched.

Eli reached across the desk and took her proffered fingers. After a quick shake, he dropped her hand like it was a live coal. A frisson of warmth had shot straight up his arm from her touch and he had no desire to examine why her touch had affected him so.

Eli stood, stoic and silent as she quickly walked out of the room, leaving the door ajar as she disappeared.

Once she was out of sight, Eli's knees gave out and he dropped into his chair. His hands shot out, catching himself on the desk when the wheels shifted.

"Did you give her the job?" Hayden leaned his grinning face inside the room and waggled his eyebrows.

Eli scowled. "No, why would I do that?"

Hayden rolled his eyes. "Because she's pretty."

Eli mimicked Hayden's eyeroll. "I can't hire someone just because they're good looking."

"Was she just after a date?"

"No," Eli grumbled and tapped his fingers on the desk. "She didn't appear to be after that at all. She sincerely seemed to want a job."

"Was she unqualified?"

Eli shrugged. "She looks like she would do fine."

"Then what's the problem."

The problem is she's stunning. And she made me feel things I didn't like. "She seems a bit young."

"How old was she?" Hayden frowned.

"Twenty-five."

Hayden scoffed. "Why the heck would that be too young?" His eyes widened after a moment. "You like her!"

Eli scowled. "I do not. I told you I've sworn off women. Not to mention I've seen plenty of beautiful women during these interviews. Looks have nothing to do with anything."

Hayden pointed his finger at his brother. "You can't not hire her because you're attracted to her."

"I'm not attracted to her. Acknowledging that someone is good looking and actually being attracted to them are two different things." Eli glared.

"Me thinks you doth protest too much," Hayden said with a raised brow.

"Don't you have a kitchen to fill?" Eli put his stoic face back on and put his eyes on his desk, refusing to look at the knowing glint in Hayden's eyes.

"You're right. Maybe I'll see if she wants to work in there instead. What was her name?"

"If she wanted to work in the kitchens, she would have put that down," Eli responded too quickly.

Hayden chuckled, and the sound became softer as he walked back down the hall. Eli sat back and tugged at his collar. *Shoot. I don't have enough real candidates as it is. I can't just not hire her because she made me feel things.* He scoffed out loud. "I sound like a woman." Shaking his head, he wrote **HIRED** at the top of her resume and put it in a small pile at the top of his desk.

IVY RESISTED THE URGE to fan herself as she walked out of the office and eventually outside to her car. Once seated in the private interior, however, all bets were off. "Whew! That man is positively sinful!" She used both hands to fan her cheeks, knowing her fair skin was flaming from the encounter.

When she felt sufficiently in charge of her body, she turned the key in the ignition and worked her way out of the parking lot. She drove slowly, admiring the resort and surrounding areas. The castle itself was stunning. Although Ivy had never seen it before the renovation, she imagined that they kept it fairly similar to what it had been originally.

Large stones made up the outer wall of the massive building. It was so wide that Ivy couldn't see any of the landscaping or forest she had heard sat on the back half of the property. But the plants in the front and the fountain that had been put in the middle of the circular driveway were plenty of eye candy.

Color greeted her everywhere she looked. It was obvious the plants were fairly new, since none of them were very large, but they still appeared to be thriving in their new environment. Azaleas and hydrangeas dripping in bright, spring blooms made a gorgeous hedge all along the cold grey of the castle walls.

Ivy knew there was a barn with horses and other outdoor equipment somewhere on the property, but she couldn't see them from where she currently was. She had also heard that the brothers had hired a landscape architect to design a garden maze. *I wonder if that's already done or still a work in progress?*

As Ivy pulled out onto the highway and turned toward her apartment, she let her mind wander. "If the back is as gorgeous as the front, I can just imagine how romantic that garden is. Mmm... a moonlit stroll on the arm of a handsome man." She smiled. "Perfect. And if that man happened to be as handsome as one, Eli Truman, then even more perfect."

Within a few minutes, Ivy pulled into her parking spot and bounced out of the car and up to her room.

"Hey, Heidi," she said as she walked in.

"Hey," Ivy's roommate answered back; her nose in a stack of textbooks. "How did the interview go?" Suddenly, Heidi's head popped up. "Did you actually get to see any of the brothers?"

Ivy felt her cheeks heat, and she turned so her roommate wouldn't see.

"You did!" Heidi jumped off the couch and shoved her glasses up her nose. "Which one did you see? Are they as handsome as the magazines say?"

With a sigh, Ivy turned around and gave a rueful smile. "I actually interviewed with Eli Truman, personally."

"Oooh, the oldest one. He always looks so suave in his business suits."

"Oh, he looks just as handsome in person. That man is hands down the most good looking guy I have ever seen. He was wearing a suit that looked like it was molded to his frame and let me tell you," Ivy pointed her finger at her roommate, "there is nothing about that man that says he sits behind a desk all day." Ivy walked over and plopped on the couch, leaning back and closing her eyes as she imagined Eli Truman in her mind. When she had first seen him, she had been knocked speechless; sure she was seeing an apparition. *No one should look that perfect.* And then when they shook hands, Ivy felt like she had touched a live wire. *He very obviously did not feel the same if his dismissal was anything to go by.*

"His hair is so dark it looks black. The top strands had that blue glow in the sunlight and his eyes," Ivy turned her head to grin at Heidi, who had sunk down beside her, "his eyes are this amazing grey tone. Cool and vivid against all that dark hair."

Heidi sighed and put her hands to her chest. "Wow. They don't make them like that anymore."

Ivy sat up straight. "What?" She gave a confused grin. "You make him sound like he's from another era."

"He's like ten years older than us, Ives. The guy is practically ancient."

Ivy rolled her eyes. "That is so dumb. Ten years isn't that big of a deal in the long run. Are you honestly telling me that if he asked you out you would say no because of a little gap in age?"

Heidi pursed her lips and tilted her head from side to side. "I don't know. Don't you think it would be awkward?"

Ivy shook her head. "Absolutely, not. What was awkward was the fact that he was a jerk through the whole interview."

Heidi's eyes shot wide open. "What?"

Ivy nodded. "Seriously. He has absolutely no sense of humor and was nearly scowling at me the whole time like I'd done something wrong. He even accused me of being too young to work there."

Heidi gasped in appropriate outrage. "He did not."

"He did."

Heidi stood and walked into their small kitchen. "Well, someday you will be grateful you look so young when the rest of us are old and wrinkly."

Ivy laughed and stood as well.

"That's a total bummer that he's a jerk though, although after his story, you really can't blame him."

Being a jerk is a choice. Ivy thought. *Lots of us have bad things happen. Doesn't mean we have to hate the world.*

"Oh, by the way, you got some mail." Heidi waved her hand toward a couple of envelopes on the table.

"Thanks," Ivy murmured, grabbing them and heading to her room to change from her interview clothes. She ripped one open and pulled out the folded papers. Once she realized what it was, she sighed. "Another bill."

Ivy added it to the ever growing pile of medical bills left from her mother's illness and subsequent death. Although, it had been a year since her mother had passed away, Ivy was still working on paying what wasn't covered by her insurance. *Sometimes it feels like I'll never get out of this hole.*

She sat down on her bed. "Hopefully, I'll get a job soon."

CHAPTER 2

"Hello, thank you for calling Avangarde Castle Resort. This is Ivy, how may I help you?" Ivy listened intently to the voice droning about their reservations before turning to the computer.

"Absolutely, let me just check on those dates for you." Ivy continued to make small talk with the person on the line while she got them the information she needed. "All right then, we'll look forward to seeing you next week. Thank you."

When she hung up the phone the clearing of a throat caught her attention.

"Oh!" She gasped when she looked up straight into the handsome face of her boss. "I'm sorry, Mr. Truman. I didn't see you there."

Ivy forced herself to breathe slowly to try to calm her rapidly beating heart. She absolutely loved working at the resort, but Mr. Truman had proved to be exactly like he showed in her original interview. He was curt and abrupt and for some reason, often seemed to be colder with her than any other staff members. Ivy worked hard and thought herself to be a model employee. Her normally sunny disposition usually helped her befriend just about everyone, so Mr. Truman's attitude bothered her. In retaliation to his emotionless demeanor, Ivy made sure she was extra polite and helpful. *Kill him with kindness. Works every time.*

However, despite his stoicism, Ivy had never been able to rid herself of the attraction she felt towards him. Whenever he was near, her face heated and her heart rate picked up. It frustrated her that she was drawn to someone so grumpy, but there was no denying the feelings.

"I noticed," Mr. Truman said in his low, crisp voice.

"Was there something you needed?" Ivy smiled her brightest smile, one that usually caused people to automatically smile back.

Mr. Truman frowned. "The coffee machine is low. I want it cleaned and filled with a fresh pot."

"Absolutely, Mr. Truman. I'll get right on that." Ivy kept her smile in place as he nodded, then turned and stalked toward his office.

"Sheesh, that man is colder than the Ice Queen," Ivy's coworker, Janet, grumbled from behind her. "Good thing he's so good looking, it almost makes up for it."

Ivy's smile dropped, and she narrowed her eyes as he disappeared. "Almost," she murmured. Turning around, she smiled again. "Guess I better go take care of the coffee. You okay up here for a few minutes?"

When the other front desk clerk nodded, Ivy headed around the counter toward the buffet in the corner.

At lunch a couple of hours later, Ivy was seated in the employee area when Denton, one of the security guards strutted in. "Hey, Ives. How's it going?" He grabbed a brown bag from the fridge and sat down across the table from her.

"Not too bad," Ivy said with a grin. "How has your day been?"

"Quiet," Denton said before stuffing half a sandwich in his mouth.

Ivy bit the inside of her cheek to keep from laughing at his manners. *Boys.* Reaching into her lunch box, she grabbed a napkin and handed it to him.

Denton grunted his thanks and wiped his mouth.

"Well, I would think a quiet day in security is a good day." Ivy stared out the window as she chewed.

Denton shrugged. "Yeah. But sometimes it's fun to have a little something to do."

Ivy turned to him and grinned. "Wishing some old granny would cause a riot? Maybe start knocking people on the head with her purse?" Ivy ate a bite of her apple. "I'll bet that would liven things up."

Denton laughed. "I'd love to see that. Maybe she'd knock some sense into Mr. Truman."

Ivy frowned. "He's not that bad," she said.

Denton raised an eyebrow. "I saw him corner you at the desk this morning. He didn't seem friendly to me."

Ivy shrugged as her attention was caught on movement outside. She watched the very man they were talking about, help an elderly woman to a bench. His smile was genuine as he held her elbow and made sure she was settled. *Why does he hide that glorious smile? How can he be so kind one minute but so cold the next?*

"Hey!" Denton snapped a finger in her face, bringing Ivy back to their conversation.

"Whoops, sorry." Ivy smiled apologetically. "I was daydreaming."

Denton chuckled. "Probably daydreaming of a place where your boss is nice."

Ivy's eyebrows furrowed. "Enough, Denton. He's an important, busy man. His stress load is probably way more than we can even imagine. He's not cruel, just... stand-offish."

Denton rolled his eyes before taking another large bite. "The guy is loaded. He doesn't even have to work, he could hire someone to do it all for him."

"Which should tell you what kind of man he is," Ivy pointed out.

Denton rolled his eyes. "Yeah, a control freak."

Ivy sighed. *Time for a change in subject.* "How did your date go last weekend? I don't think I ever heard."

Denton smirked. "Eh, she was looking for something a little more permanent than I was."

Ivy squished her lips to one side and raised her eyebrows. "Are you ever going to settle down?"

"Not if I can help it. There are way too many places to see and women to meet." Denton leaned back and rested his arm on the chair next to him. "Twenty-eight is too young to give up my life. Maybe when I'm like, forty-five."

"You'll be lucky if anyone will have you by then," Ivy teased as she stood and threw away her trash. Before Denton could come back with another smart comment, she headed toward the door. "Gotta get back at it. See ya later!"

ELI WATCHED IVY AS she walked out of the staff backroom and took her place at the front desk. She was like a bright ray of sunshine, spreading happiness everywhere she went and much to his dismay, the longer she worked at the hotel, the more he wanted to bask in her light.

She greeted her coworkers with a smile that made him want to smile back, but he forced his face to remain impassive. When a young man and woman approached the desk, he watched Ivy smile and charm her way through their conversation, getting them the help they needed. The couple went on their way with smiles on their faces.

Eli growled and stormed back to his desk, tugging on his too tight collar. "I shouldn't have hired her," he muttered to himself. He had thought that as time went on, his initial attraction to her would lessen, but the opposite had proved true. The more he watched the upbeat, beautiful redhead, the stronger the attraction grew.

He wanted to take her to dinner, wanted to spend time with her, get close to her, and especially wanted to taste those unusually full lips that taunted him at every turn. For nearly six months he had been working hard to keep her at arm's length, but for some odd reason, she wasn't as put off by his icy attitude as the other people he worked with.

Eli put his elbows on his desk and his face in his hands. He knew the workers at the hotel thought he was cold and demanding, and truth be told, he was. His divorce a couple of years ago and the following media frenzy had taught him to keep his emotions to himself. Any show of weakness could and would be held against you. Especially when it came to money hungry females.

And yet, Miss Ivy Thompson continues to smile and breeze her way through life as if nothing bad ever happens. He snorted. "She's probably never experienced heartache or real life before. Just sees the world through rose-colored glasses."

Lately, he had found himself being extra harsh with her. It was getting harder and harder to keep his distance and he had reacted by lashing out instead of giving in. Eli sighed. "I need to figure out how to handle this." He tugged on his collar again. "It's not like someone as young and vibrant as her would be interested in someone as old and grouchy as me, even if I did give in to temptation."

CHAPTER 3

"**M**r. Truman, we have a situation at the front desk," Ivy's musical voice spoke over Eli's crackling phone line.

Eli closed his eyes and soaked up the soothing tone.

"Mr. Truman, are you there?"

Eli's eyes snapped open, and he forced himself to pay attention to what she was saying. "Of course," he snapped. "What's the issue?"

"I have a customer who insists on speaking to you," she said. Eli detected a bit of hesitancy in her voice and his curiosity peaked.

"I'm on my way," Eli said before hanging up. Once out of his seat, he tugged on his jacket and straightened his tie. *What are you doing?* He shook his head and forced himself not to adjust his cufflinks. *We've talked about this. No matter how beautiful Ivy is, she's off limits. You're too old, too jaded, and made a promise to never get involved with a woman again..*

With that last thought echoing through his head, he headed out of his office and turned right, walking swiftly to the front desk. The heels of his shoes made a tapping sound on the gleaming hardwood floors as he walked across the foyer. Bright sunlight streamed in through massive front windows and reflected off a chandelier the size of a small car hanging in the great room. Eli took a deep, bracing breath as he moved, enjoying the scent of the fresh flowers scattered through the space.

The petite, redhead he was aiming for was nodding and smiling from behind the counter at an obviously elderly woman. As Eli got closer, he could see how strained her smile was, but when Ivy looked up and her eyes caught Eli's, the tension drained from her face.

Those large, green eyes lit up and her smile widened and turned genuine. "Mr. Truman, thank you for coming."

Eli clenched his fists and tightened his jaw to keep from smiling back. Instead, he forced a stiff nod and came up beside the customer.

"How can I be of assistance?" He asked; resting his right arm on the counter.

"Mrs. Gree-" Ivy began.

"You can give me the discount I was promised," the customer, a white-haired woman interrupted with a glare.

Eli frowned and looked at Ivy. Her eyes widened while she shook her head and raised her shoulders.

"I don't know what she's talking about," Ivy mouthed carefully.

"You were promised a discount?" Eli asked, turning back to the customer.

"Yes." The woman straightened and patted her hair. Her handful of rings and thick wrist of jewelry flashed in the light as her arm moved. "I spoke to someone last week on the phone and they promised that if I booked three days, I could receive a thirty percent discount."

Eli raised an eyebrow. "A thirty percent discount?"

The woman nodded. "That's what I just said, wasn't it?"

"Can you please tell me who you were talking to? That might help us figure things out."

"No, I don't have a name. I just know what they promised me." She sniffed.

"Miss Ivy, can you please bring up Mrs... ?" Eli trailed off, waiting for the woman to supply her name.

"Mrs. Greenwich," the woman stated proudly, then tilted her head and looked expectantly at Eli as if he should recognize the name.

"Mrs. Greenwich's reservation," Eli turned back toward Ivy, clearly letting the woman know he was not impressed.

"Um... well..." Ivy bit her lip and Eli's eyes followed the movement. "She doesn't have a reservation."

Eli's eyebrows shot up. He turned back toward Mrs. Greenwich. "I'm sorry, I must have misunderstood. I thought you made a reservation."

"Of course, not," Mrs. Greenwich's mouth turned down at the corners. "I don't do those type of things over the phone. Who knows how much of that information is kept private." Her eyes dropped, and she began plucking her bracelets.

She's lying through her probably false teeth. "Well, ma'am if you didn't make a reservation and don't have the name of the person you spoke to, I don't see how I can help you. We haven't run any specials lately and I don't know why someone would have offered you a discount."

White eyebrows shot down and Mrs. Greenwich's laser gaze bore into Eli. "This is no way to treat a customer. In my day and age the customer was always right."

"I'm sorry we can't accommodate your request. If you would like to book a room at regular price, you are welcome to do so. Otherwise, I would be happy to walk you to your ride."

Mrs. Greenwich gasped. "How dare you! Why you couldn't pay me to stay here!" Her nosed twitched, and she gathered her oversize purse and tugged her jacket tighter around her. Pointing a finger into Eli's face, she shook it and scolded, "I'm going to tell all my friends about how rude the staff of this place is. You can bet it will put a dent in your shabby little business here."

Eli ground his teeth, but stayed quiet. *If there's anything I've learned about the hospitality business, it's to not escalate the situation.*

"Of course," the woman sniffed, "I could be convinced to withhold my complaints..." She let her voice trail off suggestively.

Eli held in an eye roll and a sigh. "Yes, Mrs. Greenwich?"

The woman grinned and reached into her purse, pulling out a picture. "You see, I've got this granddaughter that would be just perfect for you-"

"Ms. Ivy, please see that Denton escorts Mrs. Greenwich to her car," Eli interrupted as he spun on his heel and stalked down the hallway to his office. *You've got to be kidding me!* Eli shook his head in disgust. *They're getting more and more creative, I'll give them that.*

Unfortunately, this wasn't the first time a woman had tried to set him up. It hadn't stopped happening since he and his brothers discovered the treasure in the castle. Pursing his lips and shaking his head, Eli sat down at his computer and pulled up some work documents.

"Suck it up, Eli," he scolded himself. "You should be flattered that every woman in the country seems to be after you," he grumbled sarcastically. "Or at least your money." He sighed. "Back to work."

Straightening in his chair, Eli woke his computer back up, shoved the situation with Mrs. Greenwich to the back of his mind and focused on the email on his screen.

IVY SHOOK HER HEAD slowly as she watched Denton escort the unhappy woman out of the front doors. "Geez, Louise. Will it ever stop?" She muttered. *Of course not, you ninny. Between Eli's money and his looks every single woman in the country is going to continue to hound him until he's taken. And probably even after he's taken.*

Ivy sighed. "Which only reiterates the fact that you have absolutely no chance with him," she sighed. *No matter how attractive you find him or how many times you see the kind side he keeps hidden from the public.*

She absent-mindedly re-stacked the maps of the resort sitting on the top of the counter as she pictured his grey eyes that shifted from light to stormy, depending on his mood. When she sighed out loud as she thought of his broad, firm shoulders, it snapped her out of her daydream. *You're being ridiculous, Ivy. That man would never notice someone like you, an undersized, lowly front desk clerk.* She shook her head. "Best to just forget about him," she scolded under her breath.

"What are you complaining about now?" Denton's deep voice teased from a few feet away.

Whipping around, Ivy grinned at Denton. "Hey, how did it go with the crazy matchmaker?"

Denton rolled his eyes. "Yeah, that was fun. She kept going on and on about how Mr. Truman doesn't know what he's throwing away." He shook his head and grinned. "Personally, I think any woman who has to have her grandmother set up her dates needs to reevaluate her life."

Ivy pushed her eyebrows together. "Hey now, that girl would probably be mortified if she knew what her grandmother was doing. Grandmas are notorious meddlers."

"Yeah, yeah," he put his hands up in a placating gesture. "I have one myself." He put his hands together and changed his voice to a high-pitched tone. "I only want to see you happy, Denton. I want to see my great-grandbabies before I die."

Ivy laughed. "Does she really say that?"

"Oh, yeah, almost every time we're together."

"Aw, she only does it because she loves you. Have you told her you plan to be forty-five before you settle down?"

"Of course, not. She claims her meddling is for my own good. Although, I think it's more about her than me. She just wants more grandbabies and I'm the only one available who can give them to her." He shrugged, his hands in his pockets. "So, she pesters until she gets what she wants. I don't think she'd really care who the woman was, or if I was happy."

Ivy put her hands on her hips. "Well, that's not fair. I'm absolutely sure she wants you to be happy and she definitely would care what woman you brought home."

Denton's eyebrows raised high. "If she was so concerned about my happiness, she'd quit pestering me! Her pestering makes me unhappy! And why is she so sure that marriage and babies will cure all my ills? Maybe I like being single? Maybe I'm happy that way."

Ivy raised a single eyebrow. "Are you?"

Denton shrugged and winked. "I already told you I prefer the care-free life. Nothing to tie me down."

Ivy gave an understanding smile. "Well, maybe you need to tell her that."

"Nah, it would break her heart." Denton scrunched up his face.

"Huh, I guess you'll just have to get married then."

Denton rolled his eyes. "Sorry, Ivy." His eyes twinkled with mischief. "There are too few girls like you. Until you're willing to take me on, I'll just have to stay blissfully single."

Ivy laughed, knowing he was joking. Denton was like an older brother to her and she knew he felt the same way.

"Ms. Ivy?" A stern, deep voice came from across the room.

A zing ran up Ivy's spine and her eyes shot to the glorious sound. *Oops. I shouldn't have been goofing off during working hours.* "Yes, Mr. Truman?"

Eli's eyes were boring into Denton's and he didn't answer her inquiry.

Denton cleared his throat. "Uh, excuse me." He quickly walked back to his post by the door and resumed his security stance.

Eli stalked across the room with the grace of a leopard, his eyes now trained on Ivy. *Good heavens, that man's gaze is lethal.* Her heart pounded and her mouth went dry. *Why do the forbidden things always have to be so tantalizing?*

"Ms. Ivy, next time you have an issue with someone such as Mrs. Greenwich, I would prefer you let the shift manager handle it instead of calling myself."

Ivy's cheeks burned in embarrassment. *Nothing like getting scolded by your crush to bring you back to reality.* "Uh, yes sir. I'm sorry I bothered you, sir. It's just that she asked speci-" Ivy stopped when Eli's eyes narrowed. "Nevermind, I'm sorry, sir, Mr. Truman."

Eli's mouth opened, and he paused momentarily, before shaking his head and turning back toward his office without another word.

Ivy let out the breath she was holding as his overwhelming presence dissipated with the distance. She sighed. *Will I ever get anything right with him?*.

Ivy knew all about Eli's horrible divorce a couple of years ago since it had been plastered in the newspaper for weeks after he and his brothers discovered the treasure. Even before she had met him in person, Ivy had followed his story along with the rest of the country. But after meeting him, she was even more intrigued. He might act cold and demanding toward her, but she saw how he acted when he thought no one was looking. She'd seen him escort elderly women to their cars, patch up the skinned knees of children running around the grounds and then provide lollipops and stickers for those same children. And the smile he sported while doing so, said he wasn't faking his chivalry. *Why he hides it behind this cold facade is a mystery, but maybe the right person can help break it down.*

"He needs a good woman in his life," she murmured; still watching the hallway. "Even if it isn't me." The phone rang, startling her from her drifting thoughts.

"Hello, Avangarde Castle and Resort, this is Ivy. How may I help you?" *Time to put thoughts of Eli Truman where they belong, buried in the 'forget about it' box.*

CHAPTER 4

"Heard you had a run in with an aggressive grandma," Nelson said as he burst into Eli's office.

Eli looked up with his eyes, but didn't move his head from his computer screen. "That happened several days ago. Our gossip mill must be slower than usual."

Nelson launched himself into one of the guest chairs, throwing one leg over the armrest. "Oh, I heard earlier, but I've been on an overnight horseback riding trip." Nelson raised an eyebrow. "It's nice to know you missed me so much."

Eli fought the desire to roll his eyes.

"I also heard you nearly took a security guard's head off for flirting with little, Miss Ivy." A smile twitched at the corner of Nelson's lips as he stared at his brother.

Eli stilled, then forced himself back into movement in an effort to hide his reaction. "Making sure our staff is working properly is part of my job as the hotel manager." He turned to Nelson. "My scolding had nothing to do with flirting and everything to do with the fact that he wasn't at his station."

"Sure... sure..." Nelson slowly nodded his head. "So, you don't find the red-headed fairy attractive, then?"

"I didn't say that," Eli stammered before catching himself. He could feel heat rising in his cheeks and knew he had to change the subject. "How did the trip go?"

Nelson grinned smugly. "It was fine, as usual. The weather was perfect and nobody got hurt. Win, win." He brought his leg forward and put his elbows on his knees. "Now, back to the topic at hand. I haven't seen you jealous in a long time."

31

Eli's eyebrows shot up and he had to force himself to stay seated. "I was not jealous," he snapped.

Nelson shrugged and put his hands out to the side. "Call it what you want. I say it's about time."

"What?"

"Melinda was a jerk from the beginning and I can't say I was sad to see her go." Nelson leaned back. "But Ivy. Ivy is sweet and kind and everything a stuffy dude like you needs. You should ask her out."

"You can't- I'm not- she's-"

"Take a breath, Bro." Nelson grinned. "It's not like you to be speechless, it must be more serious than I thought," he chuckled.

Eli slammed his hands down on the desk. "I'm her employer, nothing more."

"Yet. Besides, she's cute, why not ask her out?"

Eli's eyes narrowed, and he glared at his brother. "I have no interest in asking her out."

"You," Nelson pointed at Eli, "are a liar."

Eli turned back to his computer. "I think you can show yourself the way out."

Nelson stood. "Well, if you don't want her, I guess you won't mind if I take her to dinner, huh?"

Jealousy hit Eli like a sledgehammer a split second before despair set in. *That's exactly who someone as sweet as Ivy needs. Fun and outgoing Nelson would be a much better match than an older grouch like myself.*

"That's just fine, go right ahead," Eli choked out.

Nelson scoffed. "Right. I suppose you've got enough company with your superior self control." Nelson grinned and waggled his eyebrows. "But I'll bet it doesn't kiss the same as Ivy."

When Eli jumped up from his desk, Nelson took off down the hall laughing hysterically. With a groan, Eli slumped back in his seat.

"Great. Now I'm going to have to watch Ivy and my brother start dating." He rubbed the bridge of his nose. "Just what I need. Then again, maybe it will get her out of my head for good. If I can't date her, it's not like I can stop her from dating someone else." *But does that someone have to be my brother?* Eli had a sudden mental image of Ivy and Nelson kissing in front of him and he felt like the air had been stolen from his lungs. "What is wrong with you?" He growled, straightening in his seat.

"Nothing a little vacation couldn't fix," another deep voice responded from the doorway.

"Hayden! What are you doing here?"

Hayden raised an eyebrow and walked toward the seat in front of Eli's desk. "What's eating you?"

Eli cleared his throat. "Nothing. I just got done talking with Nelson."

"Ah, that explains it."

"Explains what?" Eli frowned.

"Your sour mood. I'm always cranky after I talk with the idiot." Hayden tried to brush flour off his black apron, but only smeared it into a bigger mess.

"Will you two ever grow up?"

"I did, it's Nelson that refuses to join the adult world," Hayden huffed, crossing his arms.

"Nelson runs a very successful outdoor adventure company, or have you forgotten how much he contributes to this little venture of ours?" Eli tilted his chin and gave Hayden a look.

Hayden rolled his eyes. "Oh yeah, he gets paid to ride horses, sleep in a tent and build fires. Whoop-de-do. It's so hard." Hayden pointed a finger at Eli. "Culinary school and running your own restaurant, now that's hard."

"Enough," Eli said with a head shake. "We have this argument at least once a week and I'm tired of it. Lay off your brother. Now... did you need anything in particular or were you just coming to complain about our other third?"

"I found a deal on some rare truffles in Europe that I want to order and thought to let you know to expect a bigger than normal bill for the restaurant this month."

Eli narrowed his eyes. "How much bigger than normal are we talking?"

"Nothing that we won't make back. I can charge a fortune when I use those puppies on some of my dishes." Hayden smirked.

"Whatever, just remember we're running a business, not a world market."

"Yes, Dad," Hayden groaned as he stood up.

"Oh, and it's not really me you should be telling these things to. I just hired a new accountant last week. You should tell her about the expense." Eli swiped at his screen as Hayden walked to the door.

"Which one did you hire?" Hayden paused in the doorway, leaning back into the room.

"Ms. Everwood," Eli answered.

"The blonde?" Hayden asked.

"No, that was Mrs. Summers. This one had the dark hair and blue eyes." Eli leaned back and frowned at Hayden. *Why does he care which one it was?*

Hayden scowled and stepped backwards. "Do you mean to tell me you hired the uptight one who didn't crack a smile the whole time she was here?"

Eli's eyebrows hot up. "What is it to you? She was the best qualified. I'm not hiring her to smile, I'm hiring someone to keep our numbers on track. We might have struck it rich a couple years ago, but fortunes can be found and lost in a day. Ms. Everwood interviewed well, was competent and came highly recommended."

"Yeah, and she's also got a stick up her-"

"Watch it, Hay," Eli growled. "Our mother raised us better than that."

Hayden threw his hands in the air and stomped out of the office and down the hallway.

Eli groaned and rubbed his hands over his face. "Why does he have to act like a toddler?"

"Do you really want an answer to that question?" A low, feminine voice spoke from his door.

Ah, shoot. "Ms. Everwood!" Eli felt his neck heating up. "How are you this morning?"

Cadence raised an eyebrow and strode into the room. "Fine, thank you. Even if I do have a stick where the sun don't shine." She pursed her lips and fixed her glare on Eli as she stopped in front of his desk.

I hate you, Hayden. "I'm sorry. You'll have to excuse my brother. He's..." Eli frantically searched for the right word.

"A jerk? A bit dense in the head? Uncouth?" Ms. Everwood shot out descriptions at a rapid pace.

"Passionate," Eli finally forced out over her insults.

"Passionate?" That accusing eyebrow stayed put.

"Um... yes. He tends to get worked up about things and doesn't always have much of a filter." Eli pulled on his suddenly strangling tie. "It's part of what makes him a good chef, he throws every part of him into his projects, but I apologize that he tends to forget his manners in the heat of the moment. We are actually thrilled to have you on board." Eli smiled widely at the beautiful woman in front of him.

Tall and leggy with classic features, Ms. Cadence Everwood had looks that drew the attention of men everywhere she went. Add in her dark hair and sky-blue eyes and she could stop traffic.

And yet, I feel absolutely nothing toward her. No pull, no draw, no desire to see what her plump lips taste like. An image of Ivy's pouty lips came to mind and Eli had to tug at his tie again.

"Yes, well, I suppose you can't be held responsible for your neanderthal of a brother." Cadence firmed her lips and glanced at the floor.

"Uh... thank you." *I think.* "Was there something you needed this morning?"

Cadence put the papers that were in her hand on Eli's desk. "Just bringing by some reports for you. Thought you might like to see what I've been starting on."

Eli grabbed the paper. "Great. Thank you. I will take a look at them as soon as I get the chance."

Cadence nodded and spun on her heel.

Once she was gone, Eli let out a long breath and sunk back in his seat. He rubbed his forehead, where a headache was forming. *I need to put up a 'closed' sign on my door.*

"Mr. Truman?"

Eli shot straight up in his seat at the sweet tones coming from his doorway. "Yes, Ms. Ivy?"

Ivy wrung her hands and bit her lip. Eli forced himself not to groan as he watched her. *Why are those lips so tempting?*

"I just wondered if you needed anything." Ivy continued to fidget in the doorway. "I mean, I noticed you've had a lot of people in and out this morning and I also know how you prefer to be left alone, so I wanted to see if you were doing okay. After all the visits I mean. I-" she scrunched up her face. "I guess I'm just another visit, which you probably don't want, but I was going to offer to get you a coffee, or some headache pills, or..." She trailed off. "I'm sorry. I don't really know what I'm saying. I'll just," Ivy pointed her finger down the hallway the direction she had come.

Eli sat, stunned in his chair. *She just wanted to check on me? See if I needed anything? When was the last time someone wanted to take care of me?* The thought brought up memories of his ex-wife who definitely didn't help take care of him, but had definitely wanted him to take care of her. He scowled at the memory.

"Sorry! I'm sorry. I shouldn't have interrupted." Ivy ducked her head and darted down the hallway.

Eli cursed as he shot out of his seat. "Ms. Ivy?" He chased her into the hall.

Ivy had paused mid-stride, like a rabbit frozen in the presence of a predator. Slowly, she turned back to him, but kept her face toward the floor. "Yes, sir?"

She's afraid of me. The thought sent a stabbing pain through Eli's chest. This bubbly, beautiful woman was afraid of him. "I'm sorry," Eli said softly, slowly closing the gap between them. "I'm not upset at you, I had a sudden bad thought and it showed on my face, but it had nothing to do with you."

Ivy peeked up from under her lashes, chewing on that bottom lip again.

"Fact is, I could really use that cup of coffee you mentioned. You were right, I don't like crowds and my office has been buzzing all morning. If you wouldn't mind bringing me a mug, I'd truly be grateful."

Ivy's head shot up, and she smiled at him. The force of it pulled Eli in until he was standing just inches from her.

"There's just one thing," Eli murmured, his eyes focused on those glorious lips.

The pulsing vein in Ivy's neck sped up and her breathing grew shallow. "What's that?" She whispered, her eyes never leaving his face.

Slowly, as if in a trance, Eli reached up his hand, cupping her cheek, running his thumb over her bottom lip. "Please, stop abusing this lip. I don't know how much more I can take."

Ivy's eyes widened, and she sucked in a breath.

The sound caused Eli to snap out of his daydream. He jerked his hand back like he had been electrocuted and cleared his throat. "It. I meant, I don't know how much more *it* can take. You're going to end up with a bloody lip if you keep gnawing on it the way you do," he chastised. *Great. Now you sound like her father.* Clearing his throat again, he pulled on the lapels of his coat and stood tall, feigning a coolness he didn't feel at the moment.

"O-of course." Ivy backed up a step. "Of course, that's what you meant." She smiled, but Eli could tell it was forced. "I never thought anything else. Let me get you that coffee." Ivy turned and headed toward the foyer where they had a station with drinks and snacks for their guests.

You are the world's biggest idiot. Eli berated himself the whole way back to his office where he had to fight the temptation to throw a punch through the wall. *You'll be lucky if she doesn't slap you with a sexual harrassment suit.*

WHAT IS WRONG WITH you? Ivy chastised herself as she walked on shaky legs over to the beverage station. *Quit imagining that everything he says has a romantic meaning.* For a split second, she had thought she and Eli were having 'a moment' when he had so tenderly touched her face. When his thumb ran across her bottom lip, it was like lightning had struck. Every nerve ending in her body had stood on end. *Apparently, I was the only one affected. He was just being polite enough to keep me from hurting myself.* Ivy sighed and began to chew on her bottom lip, only to force it back out of her mouth.

"Mom always did want you to break that habit," she grumbled as she poured a steaming mug of coffee. After adding two sugars and a cream, she stirred it carefully before turning and heading back towards Eli's office.

"Here you go," Ivy set down the mug carefully on the desk and backed up a few steps.

Eli didn't look at her. "Thank you." Reaching into a side drawer, he pulled out a caddy containing creamers and sugar packets.

"I already added two sugars and a creamer," Ivy hurried to explain.

Eli stiffened.

Oh, my gosh. I basically just told him that I stalk him. She wanted to groan and slap her forehead, but resisted. "I should..." She cleared her throat. "I should get back to the front desk. Is there anything else you need?" Ivy backed up all the way to the door. When he didn't answer, she made her exit. "No? I'll just leave you be, then."

Ivy rushed out of his office and made a beeline for the safety of her work station.

"Hey, little fairy, where're you coming from in such a hurry?" Nelson's playful voice made Ivy stop her mad dash and turn to face him.

"Hey, Nellie, been enjoying your little playgroup lately?" Ivy winked and walked more slowly back to her position.

Nelson put a hand to his chest in mock hurt. "Ouch. Way to shoot a man down! And I haven't even asked you out yet."

Ivy frowned. *Uh oh... Nelson knows we're just friends, right?*

Putting on his signature, million-dollar grin, Nelson put both arms on the counter and leaned into them. "So, what do you say?"

"To what?" Ivy stalled, shuffling some papers.

"A night out? A free dinner? You know... having a little fun?" Nelson tilted his head and raised an eyebrow.

"I, uh..." Ivy could feel her cheeks heating up and knew they were turning an unattractive, blotchy red. *Curse being a fair-skinned redhead.*

Nelson held up a hand before she could continue. "As friends. This is not a romantic date. I've got a few days off before my next camping trip and you've looked pretty wrung out lately. This is simply two friends enjoying a stress free evening."

Ivy put her hands on her hips. "Are you-" The phone rang, and she stopped her scolding by holding up a finger to Nelson. "Hello, Avangarde Castle and Resort. You've reached the front desk, how can I help you?"

A moment passed in silence as Ivy listened to the caller.

"Absolutely. We can have towels up to your room in a jiffy... Mm, hm... you're welcome and thank you." She pressed to end the call, only to press another extension. "Housekeeping? I need four towels sent to room two-oh-four. Thank you!" She sang out at the end as she ended the call.

Putting the phone down, she looked back at Nelson. "Where was I?"

"About to tell me how wonderful I am." Nelson pumped his eyebrows and flexed his biceps.

"Oh. Right. I was scolding you." Putting her hands on her hips she resumed her original stance. "You should never tell a girl she doesn't look good. Ever. Even if she's only a friend, she always looks fabulous," Ivy pointed a finger at him, "and don't you forget it!"

Nelson threw back his head and laughed. "All right, all right. Ivy, you have looked extraordinarily fabulous lately. Would you like to go to a totally platonic dinner with me to help you feel even more fabulous?"

Ivy pursed her lips and tilted her head from side to side, in a considering motion. "Eh, why not. I've always loved free food."

"Sheesh, way to admit you're just using me for my money!" Nelson scowled.

Ivy sniffed and began to type on the computer. "Good thing I know you don't believe that, or I'd actually feel really bad right about now."

Nelson grinned. "Good thing, I know you would feel bad or I wouldn't have joked about that to begin with." Nelson tapped the counter twice and backed away. "Meet me at Inspiration at seven." With another grin, he turned and walked through the outside doors.

"Inspiration?" Ivy made a face. "That place is super fancy. Since when is it the right place for a platonic date?" Ivy rolled her eyes and shook her head. "Boys."

CHAPTER 5

Eli rolled up his sleeves as he waited at the table for Nelson. "Not sure what was so important that we had to have a dinner meeting for it," he grumbled.

After work, Eli had been physically as well as emotionally exhausted. All he wanted was to head to his luxurious cabin on the far-side of the property and put his feet up in front of a game, while purposefully not thinking about Ivy and his conflicting feelings for her.

When she had admitted to knowing how he took his coffee, it had sent him for a loop. *Not only did she know that I was stressed from all the visitors this morning, but she knew exactly what I would need to help combat the stress.*

He shook his head. His admiration for her had skyrocketed, not to mention his attraction to her. She was obviously a nurturer, but why she bothered to nurture him, he couldn't say. *I'm just her jaded, old boss.* He huffed. "I'm almost old enough to be her father," he grumbled as he clenched the cloth napkin in his hand.

"Eli?" The feminine voice squeaked slightly, surprise evident in the tone.

Eli's head shot up. "Ms. Ivy!" He stood quickly, nearly knocking his chair over. "What are you-? I mean," He tugged on his unbuttoned collar. "How are you this evening?"

"Fine, thank you." Ivy's voice was soft and her cheeks were flushed. "I, uh," she chewed on that enticing lip and glanced around the area. "I was supposed to meet someone, but..." She looked back at him expectantly.

Eli felt a prick in his chest when he realized she was here on a date. "I see," he said gruffly before clearing his throat. "Do I know him? Can I help you find him?"

"Well, actually..." Ivy again looked around, her hands wringing in front of her.

"Did he stand you up or make you uncomfortable?" Eli felt his protective nature rise as he thought of someone throwing away or mistreating the beautiful woman in front of him. He glanced around then back at her, noting how she was dressed. *She's not really dressed like someone on a date.* He frowned as he looked at her black skinny jeans and breezy short-sleeve shirt. Her clothes had a 'casual-nice' vibe to them, not a 'I'm trying to impress a guy' vibe.

"You're welcome to wait here, if you would like. I'm just waiting on Nelson."

Ivy's eyes shot to his. "You're waiting for Nelson?"

Eli's eyebrows furrowed. "Yes. He insisted we have a business meeting tonight."

Ivy put her hands on her hips. "Really? At Inspiration? Let me guess, at seven?"

"Yes," Eli said cautiously. *She's mad. What the heck did I do?*

Ivy tapped her foot and muttered something under her breath about annoying brothers who don't leave well enough alone.

A light bulb burst to life in Eli's mind. "Did he-Did Nelson invite you here as well?" *That conniving, manipulating little-*

"Ditto whatever thoughts are going on inside your head," Ivy huffed while folding her arms.

Eli held his breath. As mad as he was at his brother, he couldn't deny that a part of him wanted to spend time with Ivy outside work, but her body language was making it clear that she was upset about the situation. *Here she was expecting Nelson and instead she got her boss.* Thinking fast, Eli walked around and grabbed the other chair and pulled it out. "Might as well take advantage of the free meal," he said with a small grin, trying to lighten the mood. "I'll make sure the bill gets back to Nelson with a hefty tip."

Warmth spread through Eli's core when Ivy smiled wide and chuckled. "Thank you," she said as she sat in the proffered seat.

Eli took his own chair. "I realize you're probably uncomfortable with this, after all, you were expecting to eat with Nelson, but you can just pretend you're having dinner with an old friend, like a father figure."

Ivy's head shot up. "Father figure? Are you kidding me?" She scowled and threw her menu down on the table. "One, you are nowhere near old enough to be a father figure to me. Two," she ticked off her fingers, "I've never seen a father as handsome as you. Three, it would be really creepy to be attracted to," she made quotations with her fingers, "'my father.'"

Eli froze at her little tirade, then sputtered. "You find me attractive?"

Ivy snapped her mouth shut, then groaned. Putting her face in her hands, she shook her head back and forth. "Me and my big mouth."

Eli chuckled and reached across the table to grab Ivy's hands. "I'm flattered," he said politely, as he pulled down her hands. "But I'm probably older than you think I am."

Ivy pursed her full lips and folded her arms across her chest. "Oh, yeah? Just how old are you, then?"

Eli felt his face heat up and he rubbed the back of his neck. "Well, I'm not actually old enough to be your father, but I am quite a bit older than you. I'm thirty-four," he admitted as he kept his eyes on his plate.

"Okay...?" Ivy's eyebrows shot up with the question.

"That doesn't make you uncomfortable?" Eli asked, surprise in his voice.

Ivy scrunched up her mouth to one side. "Why would that make me uncomfortable? We're only nine years apart. That's not a big deal."

"Really?"

"Well, I don't think so." Ivy's eyebrows furrowed as she looked at Eli. "Do you think it's a big deal?"

Eli shrugged. "I don't know, I suppose I thought a young thing like you would think I was ancient." A burst of hope exploded inside Eli's chest at the thought that Ivy wasn't opposed to their age difference, before he caught himself. *Doesn't matter. She's still far too sweet and innocent for me.*

Ivy snorted. "Hardly."

Eli fought the temptation to pull on his collar. "Well, age aside. Why don't we just enjoy a nice meal on Nelson's dime?"

Ivy grinned. "Sounds good to me."

After they had ordered their dinners, and the waitress left, silence descended upon their table. Eli racked his brain with a way to break the awkward moment, but he seemed to be tongue tied.

Ivy leaned her elbows onto the table and rested her chin on her entwined fingers. "So, Mr. Truman. Tell me about yourself." She smiled sweetly. "What did you do before you and your brothers struck it rich?"

Eli chuckled. "Please, call me Eli. Since we're here as friends, we might as well act like it."

"Okay, Eli." Ivy's voice had gone soft.

Eli wanted to mimic her actions and study her instead, but he forced himself to remember she had asked a question. He cleared his throat and put his hands in his lap. "Uh, I've always worked in hospitality. I was a shift manager at a boutique hotel down in L.A."

Ivy's mouth formed an 'O' and Eli clenched his hands as a shot of desire rang through him.

"I hadn't realized, I mean the media never said, I mean..." She trailed off, her cheeks getting brighter with every word. She swallowed hard. "I guess that explains why you are so good at your job." She smiled. "And it also makes sense as to why you three decided to open a bed-and-breakfast. Hotel manager, Chef and Recreation Enthusiast. Between you brothers, you have everything you need."

"Shift manager, not hotel manager." Eli felt the usual well of resentment swirl in his belly. "If I'd been the hotel manager, I probably would never have left," he muttered.

Ivy frowned. "Why do you say that? Didn't you want to go into business with your brothers?"

Eli shrugged as he rearranged his silverware. "Our venture started as a last ditch effort to make something of ourselves. Nelson has never been able to hold down a decent job. He kind of floated from place to place. Hayden had just been fired from his position in New York and was being blackballed through the whole city. And I had just lost half of my life savings to my ex-wife." He shrugged. "It was too expensive to stay in California." His eyes shot up into hers. "We had no other options at the time."

"Well, it looks like it all worked out!" Ivy grinned and then her face fell. "Although, I'm sorry those things happened to you. It must have been terrible to have lost your wife at the same time your brother lost his job."

Eli reached out and patted her hand. Her skin felt silky and warm and he pulled back quickly before his mind came up with other things to do with that skin. "It was a long time ago, don't worry about us. We're pretty happy with our circumstances."

Ivy giggled. "Yes, I suppose the 'Overnight Billionaire Bachelors' would be pretty content."

Eli groaned and scrubbed his face with his hands. "That was the dumbest name ever."

"Well, most of America must not think that, since it seems to bring the women to the hotel in droves. Last I looked at the demographics, we have an abnormally high amount of single women who stay at the resort." Ivy smiled, but it didn't reach her eyes.

Hmm... could she possibly be jealous? He snorted. *That's ridiculous. She may have admitted she found me attractive, but that doesn't mean she wants more than friendship.* "Yes, well, I'm afraid they are going to find themselves disappointed. At least with me. I have no plans to remarry again."

Ivy's face grew pale. "Never? But you're so young," she whispered.

"Once was enough," Eli stated bluntly.

"Was it really that awful? Didn't you love your wife at all when you married her?"

Eli fought the temptation to roll his eyes. "I suppose I did at one point. But she cured me of that fairly quickly. She was," he glanced at Ivy then back down at his hands, "very beautiful. Everything you would imagine in a California girl."

Ivy's face fell and Eli immediately felt bad.

"Sorry. You don't want to hear all this."

"Yes, actually, I do." Her eyes were sad, but she mustered up a small smile. "That is, if you're willing to tell me."

Eli sighed and ran a hand through his hair. "She was a sweet talker, and I fell for it hook, line and sinker. But after we were married, I realized she wasn't all she appeared to be. She wanted more than I could give her on my meager salary. It was never enough. I was never enough and eventually she ran out of patience."

"Oh, Eli," Ivy voice broke. "How horrible. I'm so sorry." Her hand reached across the space only to hover for a moment before pulling it back. "She doesn't know what she lost."

Eli barked a laugh. "As kind as that thought is, I definitely got the better end of the deal. Now I'm set for life and she probably ran through our life savings in the first month of our separation." Eli knew he sounded bitter and hateful, but he couldn't seem to help his tone. Melinda had chewed him up and spit him out and a part of him hoped that when news broke of his success, she had regretted what she had done.

Ivy's eyes glowed with unshed tears. "I see," she whispered.

Is she crying for me? There's no way. Eli's eyebrows lowered, and he frowned at the emotion on Ivy's face.

With obvious effort, Ivy pulled herself back together and sat taller in her chair. "Oh, look, our meals are here." She smiled at the waitress and thanked her as her plate was set down.

"Thank you," Eli murmured when his own plate was put in front of him. He couldn't take his eyes off Ivy. *Why was she so upset about my divorce?* He finally looked down and began to eat his meal. *She probably just doesn't like to hear sad things. Someone as upbeat as Ivy has probably never experienced the darker side of life. Just another reason why the two of us would never work.*

"THANK YOU FOR WALKING me to my car," Ivy worked hard to keep her smile in place. She was devastated that her evening with Eli was coming to an end. *This is probably the only date I'll ever get with him. And yes, I'm counting it as a date, even if Nelson did set us up.* She said firmly in her mind, trying to quiet the negative voice in the back that was attempting to ruin her fun.

"Of course," Eli replied. His deep voice was soothing and Ivy loved to listen to it. "Have a safe drive home," he said with a nod before spinning on his heel and walking across the parking lot.

Ivy's shoulders slumped and she let out a long sigh. Grabbing her keys out of her purse, she unlocked it and slid behind the wheel. "Well, that went well," she muttered as she drove home. "I don't know whether to strangle Nelson or thank him." She twisted her lips to the side. "On one hand, I got to have dinner with Eli Truman." She grinned. "On the other hand, I got to hear about his gorgeous California wife who ran off with all his money." She pursed her lips and blew a stray hair out of her face.

"At least I know the full story behind why he's so cold to people." She chewed her bottom lip. "And why he won't even look at the women who come to the resort." She rested her head on her hand, with her elbow on the window ledge. "Which means I don't have to watch him hook up with someone else, but it also means he has no intention of hooking up with me." She rolled her eyes at herself. "He wouldn't give you the time of day anyway, Ivy," she scolded. "Didn't you pay attention to what he was attracted to? A California girl. That means legs that go on for miles, tan skin and flowing blonde hair. Basically, everything you're not."

Ivy sighed heavily. "Best to just get it through your thick head now. If he had any interest in you, he would have mentioned it when you were stupid enough to blurt out that you thought he was handsome. Not to mention, he only touched you once all night, and that was to pat your hand like a child." She pinched her lips. "It's like he thought I had a disease or something." With a small growl, she sat up taller in her seat and straightened her shoulders. "Be grateful you had one date even if it was a blind set-up. It's more than most girls get with him." With a firm nod, she pushed the thought of Eli Truman out of her head and pulled into her parking spot at her apartment building.

"Time to focus on getting out of debt and going to college, not your unattainable boss."

CHAPTER 6

"So, how'd it go?" Nelson asked with a cocky grin as he strode into Eli's office the next morning.

Eli glared at his youngest brother. "I should give you a black eye for what you did last night."

Nelson rolled his eyes. "Oh, please. You've been watching that girl since she got here. It's obvious to anyone who pays attention that you're attracted to her. You should be thanking me for setting you two up when you obviously didn't have the courage to do it yourself."

"Has it ever occured to you that I didn't want to be set up? That I have no desire to date anyone? That I'm perfectly content being a bachelor the rest of my life?" Eli found himself gripping the arm rests on his chair to keep from strangling his brother. *He has no right to meddle in my life.*

"Nope," Nelson popped the 'P' at the end and grinned. "Ah, come on man, everyone knows that out of the three of us boys, you're the family man. You need a white picket fence and a couple of kids sitting on your knee. You've always been the responsible one." Nelson crossed one leg over the other. "We also knew that Melinda was never going to be the one to give that to you. She's was a piranha from the beginning, you were the only one who didn't see it."

Eli chose to ignore Nelson's comment about him being a family man. His dream of a wife and children had died years ago. "Well then, you would be glad to know that I've learned my lesson and have no intention of ever getting close to a woman again. Besides," he continued before Nelson could say anything, "Ivy has no interest in an old, jerk of a man who also happens to be her boss."

Nelson's eyes widened, and he sprang upright from his slumped position. "She said that? Are you serious?"

"N-no," Eli stammered. "But why would she? I'm quite a bit older than her and everyone knows I'm not nice. She's young and sweet and naive. She's probably never had anything bad happen to her in her life."

Nelson's jaw dropped. "Didn't you get to know her at all while you guys were at dinner?"

Eli stiffened. "What do you mean? We talked, I told her about us and how we ended up here at the resort."

"But did you ask questions about her?"

"Uh, no." Eli felt a pang of regret hit him. *Did I spend the whole evening complaining about my former life and never give her the chance to speak? Maybe that's why she was near tears, not because she felt bad for me, but because I wouldn't shut up.*

"You are a complete dolt." Nelson shook his head and stood.

"You're one to talk. She thought she was meeting you at that dinner, did it ever occur to you her feelings were hurt when you stood her up?" Eli's defenses were up and he didn't appreciate Nelson making him out to be the bad guy. *Nelson is the one who started all this in the first place.*

Nelson laughed as he walked to the doorway. "Jealous and a dolt. What a combination." He let the door slam shut behind him.

Eli rubbed his temples. "Life just keeps getting better and better." Reaching into his desk drawer he pulled out a bottle of pills and swallowed a couple, trying to head off his threatening headache.

For the next couple of hours, Eli struggled to concentrate on his work. Nelson's accusations and Ivy's face kept swimming in front of his vision. *Am I being stupid for not trying for more? Is there more to Ivy than I discovered last night?* "I really don't know anything about her except what was on her resume," he murmured, staring blankly at his computer screen.

He thought back to when he spoke of his ex-wife and felt a sharp pain in his chest at Melinda's deception. "That," he growled, as he rubbed the spot, "that is why I won't do it again."

Even though it had been nearly two years, the pain of the separation and Melinda's abandonment still hurt. Eli had learned to deal with the hurt, he had learned how to put aside his emotions and act as if he was unaffected, but truthfully, he had never fully gotten over the pain of what she had put him through.

"Women aren't worth it. Not even ones as sweet as Ivy." His fists were clenched and his nostrils flared. "I'll just have to stay away from her. I can't afford to give her the wrong impression. Let Nelson call me names, I know first hand what happens when you allow yourself to fall for someone and I won't do it again."

Using the fierce self-discipline Eli was known for, he pushed thoughts of the perky, ginger out of his mind and threw himself into his work; determined not to give in to any more daydreams.

CHAPTER 7

She's everywhere. Eli had the fleeting thought that maybe he was being haunted. The more determined he was to keep Ivy out of his mind, the more he saw her. When he went to the kitchen to refill his coffee, instead of using the station in the lobby, she was in there replenishing the cookies they kept at the front desk.

When he chose to eat his lunch in his office to avoid seeing anyone, her laughter echoed through the hallway, immediately giving him a different type of hunger.

When he parked at the side entrance to the castle, instead of the back, she was there unlocking all the doors.

He couldn't seem to get away from her bright smile and cheerful attitude, or the desire to kiss those full, pink lips. "At least, she doesn't appear to be as bothered as I am," he grumbled. "Looks like our little dinner awhile back didn't affect her the same way it did me. Thank heavens for small miracles."

Sitting at his desk that afternoon he felt overwhelmed by his thoughts of her. "What is wrong with you?" He growled while pushing his hand through his hair. "You can't have her and you need to get used to the idea."

"Mr. Truman?" Ivy's soft, tentative voice interrupted his scolding.

Eli jerked out of his seat. "Ms. Ivy! I'm sorry... I didn't see you there." He cleared his throat. "Won't you come in?" *Wait, what? Why am I inviting her in?*

Ivy stepped cautiously into the room. It was clear she was nervous as she wrung her hands in front of her and she struggled to make eye contact with Eli.

"What can I do for you?" Eli sat down and rested one arm on his desk, turning his body toward her. His eyes drank in her beautiful, red hair flowing around her shoulders and the lip gloss that highlighted his favorite part of her face. Even her slacks and polo, which were their standard uniform for the hotel, couldn't detract from her beauty.

"Umm... I know you told me to approach the shift manager next time someone asked for you, but I'm afraid this woman isn't having it." Ivy shrank into herself, ducking her face into her shoulder as if afraid he would yell at her.

"What are you talking about?" Eli frowned.

"There is a woman at the front desk asking, well, demanding is more like it, to speak to you." Ivy bit her lip. "I tried to pass her off to the shift manager, but she threw a fit and disturbed the whole lobby. She insists you are the only one who can help her." Ivy sighed and put up her hands. "I can get security to escort her out if you want, but I wanted to see what you thought before I went that far."

Eli fought the temptation to roll his eyes. He settled for rubbing against the furrow in his forehead. "How old is this one?"

"I'd guess in her twenties."

Great. Not matchmaking then, simply here for herself. "Did she give any clue as to what she wanted?"

Ivy's mouth thinned and her jaw clenched.

Eli's eye narrowed as he watched her display of temper with interest. *I've never seen her get upset.*

"You." Came the curt response.

Is she jealous? Eli raised a single eyebrow and Ivy dropped her eyes to the floor. *Maybe she was more affected by me than I thought.* Standing, he pulled his suit jacket from the back of his chair and pulled it on, straightening his tie and shirtsleeves. "Thank you, Ms. Ivy. You made the right decision to come get me." He walked over to the doorway. "After you," he waved an arm toward the hallway.

Ivy looked stiff as she marched down the hallway toward the front lobby and Eli couldn't help the smirk that curled one side of his mouth. Seeing Ivy in a snit over another woman gave Eli some much needed insight into the woman he couldn't get out of his head.

As they got closer to the front desk, Eli fought the urge to throw back his head and groan. *Here we go again.*

A woman in a short, tight skirt and high heels was looking into a compact mirror and fluffing her hair as they approached. When she noticed them, she slammed the mirror shut, stuffed it in her purse and pushed her lips out into a seductive smirk.

"Ms. Samuelson, this-"

"I'm Angelica," the woman interrupted Ivy and put her hand out toward Eli. She had the back of her hand up as if she expected him to kiss it.

Eli frowned at her forwardness, but took her hand and gave it a small shake before letting go.

He nearly smiled when he heard Ivy smother a giggle at Ms. Samuelson's obvious disappointment.

"Eli Truman," Eli responded to her introduction with a nod.

"Oh, I know who you are," Ms. Samuelson purred. "Everyone does." She reached into her purse and pulled out a notebook and pen. "I run the award winning blog, 'Much Ado About Everything.'" She raised her eyebrows expectantly.

Eli gave a blank stare.

Ms. Samuelson cleared her throat delicately. "Yes, well, I'd like to interview you for the blog." She gave a wide smile, showing off her perfect, white teeth. "The women who read my words are dying to know more about you." She leaned in close and twerked an eyebrow. "I like to get the more... intimate details that newspapers leave out."

"I see," Eli murmured.

Smiling brightly, Ms. Samuelson hooked her arm through Eli's. "Let's go somewhere more private, shall we?" She started to take a step, but Eli didn't budge.

"I'm afraid, Ms. Samuelson," Eli started as he unhooked her arm, "That I'm far too busy to grant you the interview you're asking for."

"I see," Ms. Samuelson narrowed her eyes and studied him for a moment. "How about Friday night then? I know a wonderful little restaurant in the next town over."

"I'm sorry, I have an appointment Friday night." Eli tugged on his suit jacket, hoping this woman would get the hint without him having to be rude.

"You work on Friday evenings?" Her sculpted eyebrows were high on her forehead.

"No, it's a... social engagement." Eli inwardly cringed when he heard Ivy softly gasp in the background.

"You mean a date?" Incredibly, her eyebrows shot even higher. "The rumor mill says you don't date at all, Mr. Truman. Just who is this date with?"

Eli scowled. "That is none of your business. I think it's time you left Ms. Samuelson." Turning, Eli gave a nod to Denton who began walking over to their little pow-wow.

With a sniff, Ms. Samuelson stuffed her notebook back in her purse and straightened her shoulders. "No need to call the dogs over, Mr. Truman. I heard you loud and clear." Without another word, she stalked toward the front doors and out into the parking lot.

Good riddance. Eli felt the tension in his shoulders release ever so slightly at her leaving. The elation he felt at the departure was quickly replaced with guilt when he turned and caught Ivy looking at him with a crestfallen expression.

When she caught his eye, she quickly blinked, schooling her emotions and pasted a fake smile on her face. "I'm so sorry about her, sir.

Reporters don't always know where the boundaries are. Or bloggers in this case."

"Maybe so, but she was right about one thing. I don't date."

Ivy's eyebrows pushed together. "But you said you had one Friday night."

Eli pushed his hand through his hair. "I said I had a social engagement. She just assumed it was a date."

"So, you're not going out with someone?"

Is it my imagination or does she sound relieved? Eli eyed her for a moment, debating whether he should cross that line or not. He had tried so hard to stay away from her but fate or whatever you wanted to call it, seemed to have other plans. No matter how hard he tried, he couldn't get her out of his head. And he found himself more and more attracted to her as time went on, not less.

"Well, I will be if you say yes." Eli said plainly.

Ivy frowned and cocked her head. "I don't understand."

Eli straightened. "Ms. Ivy, will you help me not be a liar by going to dinner with me this Friday?"

Ivy's bright green eyes widened and her mouth dropped open. "I... I don't know what to say."

A small smile played on Eli's mouth. "I think most women would say yes."

"Is that what you're hoping I'll say?" Ivy was watching him curiously and Eli wished he could read her thoughts.

Have I read her wrong? She admitted out loud she was attracted to me and that our age difference doesn't bother her. And I could have sworn she was jealous of Ms. Samuelson a few moments ago? Maybe I've been out of the game too long. He rubbed his forehead. "Well, I-"

"I'd love to!" Ivy blurted out quickly.

Eli's eyes shot to her and he cheered internally at the blush covering her cheeks. "Thank you. I'll send you the details." Feeling uncomfortable and unsure of what more to say, he spun on his heels and hurried back to his office. *Come on, man. It's just a little dinner date. You and Ivy ate together a couple of weeks ago and did fine. You can do it again.*

IVY FELT AS IF SHE were in a fog as she watched Eli walk back to his office. *He did it. He actually asked me on a date.* She frowned for a moment. *Well, sort of. But still, he could have asked any girl to help with his cover story and he didn't.* "He asked me," she whispered to herself, a small smile creeping onto her face.

The longer the thought pulsed through her brain, the more excited she became. *A dinner with Eli Truman. Not a set up. Not a blind date. A real dinner date.* "Oh my gosh, oh my gosh," Ivy did a little celebratory hip wiggle and bit her lip to keep her smile from getting any bigger.

Maybe, this is my chance. Could he possibly see me as more than an employee?

The day passed in a blur as Ivy went about her job on auto pilot. Her mind swirled with ideas of how to get Eli to step out of his cold, CEO persona and let down his guard enough to let Ivy see the real him. The him that helped elderly customers, the him that smiled with genuine warmth, the him that made sure the people at the resort were taken care of to the best of his abilities.

"Maybe, what he needs more than a woman is just a friend." She chewed her lip as she recorded some information on the computer. "Can I just be his friend?" *It would be better than nothing.* She thought, even as the thought hurt her heart. Being close like that would definitely be a sweet form of torture. *But he's made it plain he doesn't wasn't anything more.* Firming her decision in her mind, Ivy nodded to herself. *Friends it is... for now.*

CHAPTER 8

E li pulled up in front of Ivy's apartment complex and took a deep breath. "It's not really a date. Just a social engagement between two adults. She's helping with your cover story." Unfortunately, sweat still beaded on his hairline and his heart was racing in his chest. Obviously, his body hadn't gotten the message.

With a growl of frustration at his nervousness, he stormed up to Ivy's door and pounded on it. *Pull it back a notch, man. You're going to scare her.* Forcing his clenched fist to relax, he let his arms hang by his side.

The door squeaked slightly when it opened. "Oh," a medium-height brunette stood in the doorway. Her mouth was open and her eyes wide.

"Is Ivy here?" Eli said with forced politeness. *What exactly is she staring at?*

"Of course," the girl gulped. "Let me grab her."

"I'm here!" Ivy's musical voice enveloped Eli and his muscles involuntarily relaxed. "Sorry, I was grabbing my purse," she said with a smile as she finished walking to the doorway. "Thanks, Heidi, I'll be back in awhile."

"Okay," Heidi breathed while watching Eli and Ivy walk to the car.

"Let me," Eli opened the passenger side door for Ivy and took her hand to help her sit. She looked divine in her pencil skirt and flowy blouse. The green of her blouse brought out the gem tone in her eyes and made them sparkle. But it was her high heels and legs that had Eli's attention as she sat and swung her body into the car.

"Thank you," Ivy murmured as she wiggled to settle herself on the soft, leather.

Eli nodded, unsure he could answer without sounding tongue-tied, and pushed the door closed. He pulled on his collar as he walked around the car, trying to loosen the noose at his neck. *Not a date, not a date.*

"Sorry about my roommate," Ivy said with a chagrined expression. "She thinks you're a celebrity, so I guess I shouldn't have been too surprised at her flop-jawed response to meeting you."

"A celebrity? Really?" Eli grinned, amused at the girl's image of him.

"Well, to be fair, she's never met you in person, but has seen you all over the media for the last two years, so what else was she to think?" Ivy raised a teasing eyebrow.

Eli shrugged. "You don't seem to view me as a celebrity."

Ivy gave a light laugh, and the sound sent warmth through Eli's chest. "I work for you. Kind of bursts the whole bubble."

Eli put a hand to his chest in an offended manner. "Madam! Are you suggesting I don't act like a rich, famous snob?"

Ivy's laugh was louder this time. *What is it about that sound?*

"More like a rich, grumpy man." Ivy's words were said with a smile to let him know she was teasing.

Eli humphed. "I guess I am grumpy sometimes," he muttered.

Ivy reached over and put her hand on his forearm. "You can be a little intimidating, but none of us who know you are put off by it. I know you're just trying to protect yourself."

Eli had frozen at her touch. Even the smallest touch of her fingers sent his pulse to racing like a horse at the Kentucky Derby. "What do you mean?" He finally choked out.

"You told me the story of your divorce. And now the press is all over you three brothers like a swarm of locusts." She shrugged. "I'm pretty sure I'd be stand-offish, too."

A slow smile tugged at Eli's lips. "Thanks, I think." He said with a small shake of his head.

"You're welcome," Ivy sang out as she smiled at the scenery they were passing. "So, where are we going to eat tonight?"

Suddenly, Eli felt like a teenager on a date with his first crush. "Um, I thought we might go to Newark's?" His voice rose at the end like a question instead of a statement. For some inexplicable reason, he desperately wanted to please her.

Ivy's eyes widened, and she gaped at him for a moment. "Really? Newark's? Whoa..." Her voice trailed off.

"Is that a good whoa, or a bad one?" Eli held his breath as he glanced sideways at her.

"Definitely a good one. I've never even come close to eating somewhere like Newark's. It's waaayyy above my paygrade."

Eli frowned. *We've barely begun the evening, and she's already angling for a pay raise?*

A loud slap caught his attention. Ivy sat slumped forward with her hand on her forehead. "Oh, my gosh. I can't believe I just said that to you. I seriously meant it as a joke, but because you're my boss, it sounded way wrong." Her large, green eyes were repentant when they turned toward Eli. "I'm so sorry. I love my job and was definitely not trying to make a complaint. I was just throwing out a cliche, but didn't stop to think about who I was with. Sometimes the filter from my brain to my mouth takes a nap. A very long, hibernating, doesn't-wake-up-until-spring nap."

"It's all right," Eli said stiffly. Her pale face and desperation in her voice let him know she was sincere in her apology. *Ivy isn't like the other girls, let it go.* "You, uh," he motioned to his forehead. "You have a handprint on your..."

Ivy pulled down the visor mirror and gasped. "Wow. I hit myself harder than I thought." She giggled. "Probably serves me right after a comment like that." She pursed her lips and turned back towards the scenery. "With my lack of tact, I'll be lucky if you don't fire me by the end of the night."

Eli frowned. *She thinks I'm going to fire her? Is that what she really thinks of me?* He thought back to how he often spoke sharply at the office and suddenly he felt about two feet tall. "I'm sorry," he said quietly. "I have no intention of firing you and I'm sorry you feel like that's a possibility. Truth is, I would really like to enjoy tonight. Do you think we could start over?" He pulled into the restaurant parking lot and turned off the car. "Tonight, I'm not your boss. Just a friend who asked you to dinner."

Ivy looked stunned for a moment before a wide smile crossed her face. "I would love that," she said breathlessly.

That same warmth that Eli had felt several times around this woman, again pulsed through his chest. He fought the urge to rub his fingers across the spot. The desire to pull her into his arms was so strong it scared him. *I barely know her. She'd think I was crazy if I pulled something like that.*

Clearing his throat, he said, "stay put for a moment," then stepped out and crossed to her side of the car. Holding her door, he reached out a hand to help her rise.

"Thank you," she murmured. Her pouty lips were slightly curled at the ends and her shining eyes looked at him as if he were a hero.

"You're welcome," he responded automatically. Once Ivy was out of the car, Eli kept hold of her hand and tucked it into his arm before shutting and locking the car. He glanced down at her while they walked and noted that her cheeks had turned bright pink and she was having trouble meeting his gaze. *Either she's never had a guy show her decent manners before, or she really is attracted to me like she said.*

The first thought angered him but the second thought send a ping of hope into his heart. "After you," he said politely, holding open the door.

"Thank you," Ivy said again. Once they got inside the restaurant, Ivy stopped. Her jaw dropped slightly as she looked at the elegance around her. "It's even better than I imagined."

Eli followed her gaze and tried to see things through her eyes. Having worked in hotels his whole life, he had spent most of his days surrounded by opulent excess, but he had to agree that the restaurant was impressive. A massive, crystal chandelier hung in the lobby, twinkling in the surrounding lights. Its prisms swung slightly from the air conditioning, causing rainbows to dance on the ceiling and walls.

Rich, dark carpets led a path through the foyer and into an elegant dining hall. The whole building had an 'old-world wealth' feel to it. The smell of spice and cooking meats assaulted his senses, reminding him he was there to eat, not just gawk.

"Mr. Truman," a sharp voice called from the right. "Thank you for joining us tonight."

Eli turned toward the maitre'd and nodded. "Hello, Steve."

"We have your normal table all ready for you, Mr. Truman. If you'll just follow Elizabeth." Steve nodded toward a pretty woman who appeared to be in her twenties.

"Right this way, Mr. Truman," Elizabeth said with a sunny smile. She walked quickly into the restaurant, her high heels clacking on the hardwood after they stepped off the carpets.

Eli rested his hand on Ivy's lower back and guided her after the hostess. Glancing down, he saw that Ivy's face had gone from one of awed joy, to one that appeared sad. Eli frowned. *What in the world happened between the front door and here to upset her?*

Elizabeth stood at a small table that was set up next to the large picture windows that spanned half of the restaurant. Smiling wide, she swept her hand toward the table. "Will this do, Mr. Truman?"

"This is great, thank you, Elizabeth," Eli said quickly, still looking at Ivy's downcast face. He forced a grin at the hostess, dismissing her, as he stepped up to pull out Ivy's chair.

"Thank you, again," Ivy said.

"You're welcome, again." Eli leaned down and whispered the last part in her ear. He forced himself not to grin when he watched a delicate shiver run through her, as he walked around to his seat.

"Can I get you anything else, Mr. Truman?" Elizabeth chirped from his side.

Eli jumped a little, not having realized the hostess was still there. He looked up at the overeager woman. "No, thank you." He looked at Ivy, who was staring out the window. "We're fine."

"Just let me know if that changes," Elizabeth raised a single eyebrow, then sashayed back towards the front.

Eli immediately turned his attention back to his guest. "Are you okay?" He leaned across the table.

"Yes. Sorry," Ivy toyed with her napkin.

"You don't look okay. Did I do something?"

"Oh, no." Ivy looked up at him. "You have been wonderful." She bit her lip. "I've never had someone open doors and offer me their arm before." She gave a shy smile. "It's nice to know that chivalry isn't dead. I just..." She scrunched up her face and pushed her lips from side to side.

"Do you want to go somewhere else to eat?" *Maybe she doesn't like this kind of food?*

"This place is gorgeous, I just..." She sighed and ran a hand through her hair. "I just can't compete," she stated, looking Eli dead in the eye.

"Compete? What are we competing for?" His eyebrows furrowed together and his nose wrinkled.

"With the likes of her." Ivy waved a hand toward the front of the restaurant.

"Her? Her who?"

"Elizabeth," Ivy said, exasperation evident in her voice. Her head tilted to the side, and she purposefully widened her eyes as if he should know exactly what she was talking about.

"The hostess? Why are we competing with her?" Eli shook his head. *Why doesn't she just say what she means?*

Ivy sighed. "We're not competing with her. Just me. I can't compete with tall, elegant, gorgeous women who obviously want you."

Eli jerked back. "You think I'm interested in the hostess?"

Ivy threw up her hands. "Who wouldn't be? There's no way you didn't notice how she was looking at you. She never looked or addressed me once, did you notice that? Not to mention how she looked herself." Ivy then motioned to herself. "I can't compete with that. I'm short, uncultured and average. I can't compete with Miss Bedroom Eyes over there."

Eli closed his eyes and chuckled for a moment before looking back at Ivy. She looked affronted at his laughter and he was quick to reach across the table and grab her hands. "Ivy, I'm sorry for laughing. Truth is, I didn't even notice what the hostess was wearing, let alone how she was looking at me. Her, 'bedroom eyes' as you call them, were completely lost on me. I meant it when I said I don't date. Other than some business meetings, I haven't been on a date with a woman since I got divorced. And if you hadn't noticed," he cleared his throat and pulled his hands back, "I think you're absolutely lovely. I wouldn't have asked you here tonight if I thought otherwise." He tugged at his collar, feeling the heat from his words traveling up his neck.

"Are we on a date, then?" Ivy asked softly. "Or is this still just a cover for your excuse to that blogger?"

Eli didn't answer right away. *Is this a date? Yes, I used the blogger as an excuse, but I've been wanting to ask her out for months. Does this count? Am I ready to open that can of worms?* His thoughts swirled, and he wasn't sure what was the right path to take. He finally decided to be as honest as he could. "I don't know."

Ivy narrowed her eyes and studied him for a moment. "Fair enough," she replied with a nod. Smiling, she picked up her menu and began studying the options in front of her.

Eli slowly exhaled, feeling his body relax at her acceptance of the situation. "Everything I've ever eaten here has been fantastic, so feel free to get wild with your choice of entree." Eli winked as he picked up his own menu.

Ivy laughed loudly, then quickly quieted down and covered her mouth. "Oops. Sorry. I probably shouldn't be so loud in a place like this."

Eli was sad she had toned down her amusement. Her laugh was musical and when she threw back her head, it showed off the smooth length of her neck. Annoyed, he glanced around, noting a few faces had turned their direction. "Nah, don't worry about it. They're probably gawking at me rather than you. I tend to cause a spectacle when I go out and about."

"Even after two years, people are still trying to get a glimpse of a Truman brother, huh?" Ivy grinned, but it looked slightly strained.

"I suppose so," he grumbled. "Did you find anything that sounded good?" He asked in order to change the subject.

"Yep." Ivy grinned. "The salmon looks wonderful. How about you?"

Eli nodded slowly. "I was thinking more along the lines of a lobster tail. Have you ever had one?"

Ivy's eyes were wide as she slowly shook her head. "Uh, nope. Way out of a college kid's budget."

Eli nearly choked. "You're in college?" This time it was Eli who was louder than was appropriate in the quiet restaurant.

Ivy ducked her head and her cheeks turned a fiery pink. "Sort of." She cleared her throat.

"Are you two ready to order?"

Both Eli and Ivy snapped their attention to the server who had approached their table.

"Thank you, yes," Eli said softly. His eyes went to Ivy, and he raised his eyebrows, deferring to her.

"I'll take the salmon, please," Ivy said with a smile.

"And I'll have the lobster," Eli's eyes never left Ivy's as he handed his menu back and the server left. "Now, tell about your being a student. I'm surprised I didn't know that. Are you doing a graduate degree of some kind?"

Ivy fiddled with the silverware in front of her. "No. Nothing like that." She glanced up at Eli from beneath her eyelashes then back down at her plate. "I've only taken a couple of online classes. I haven't made much progress, but I hope to someday."

"Why didn't you head out straight from high school?" Eli's eyebrows were scrunched and his lips turned down in a frown.

"Ah," Ivy gave a short, hesitant laugh. "Life just didn't turn out that way." Her pink cheeks and the fact that she wouldn't meet his eyes let Eli know she wasn't telling him something. *It's not really any of my business, though.*

Eli sat and studied her for a minute. "What's stopping you from going now?"

"I'm uh, I'm saving up until I can pay for tuition." Her eyes continued to focus on the tablecloth.

"Why not just take out a student loan?"

Ivy's face paled and Eli found himself confused. *Why is this such a big deal? College kids deal with these kinds of things every day.*

"I'd really prefer not to go into debt, at least until I absolutely have to," Ivy finally met his gaze. The jut of her chin spoke of confidence and determination but her eyes were an open book, and they told a more vulnerable story. Eli found himself even more intrigued, but forced himself to drop the topic.

"That's a good plan. Most people borrow money without batting an eye."

"Really?" Ivy beamed. "Most people tell me I'm being ridiculous."

Eli chuckled and folded his arms across his chest. "If it's what you want, then who cares what they think. It's your life and your timeline. What are you planning to study?"

Ivy shrugged. "Nothing too exciting. Business management."

Eli mimicked her shrug. "You can't go wrong with that. It can be used in all sorts of careers."

"That's what I thought, too. Especially since I didn't have any kind of amazing talent or passionate, driving desire for something else."

Eli reached over and stilled Ivy's fidgeting hands. "Most of us are just normal people, Ivy. And there's absolutely nothing wrong with that. I mean, we're all unique in small ways, but the vast majority of the population will never stand out and be recognized for anything out of the ordinary. Truthfully, a quiet life is nothing to sneer at."

Unconsciously, Eli began to rub his thumb over the smooth skin of her hand as his gaze drifted to the window. The mood at the table had become reflective and somber.

"Do you regret your time in the limelight?" Ivy tilted her head, her gaze curious.

Eli turned back to face her and gave another shrug. "I don't know. Sometimes. I mean, starting up the resort would have been a lot harder, it would have taken a decade to get to where we are now, with it all fixed up and such. But all the attention, the aggressive women and media frenzy..." He scrunched his nose. "Not my cup of tea."

Biting her lip, Ivy turned her hand over and let their hands meet palm to palm. "I'm sorry. Although, I sympathize, I can honestly say I have never found a billion dollars in my basement and had to deal with the fall out."

Eli gave a small, amused grin before his eyes fell to their hands. His fingers had stopped moving, but he couldn't seem to pull himself away. He sucked in a quick breath as she began to toy with his fingertips. No words were spoken or needed as they watched each other. Electricity crackled around them and Eli began to wonder why he had ever fought something so wonderful in the first place.

BY THE END OF THE MEAL, Ivy had cleaned her entire plate, plus shared a dessert with Eli, but there was no recollection of what anything tasted like. After she and Eli had held hands, the chemistry between them had skyrocketed and Ivy's brain had never recovered.

She floated through the meal in a fog of happiness and contentment. After Eli had paid their check, he came around and pulled out her chair for her. "Thank you," she said with a wide smile. *Who pulls out a woman's chair any more?*

"Of course," Eli answered with a smile of his own. Turning sideways, he offered his arm.

Biting her lips between her teeth to contain the twitterpated smile trying to split her face, Ivy put her hand inside the crook of his arm and walked with him through the restaurant.

Her happy bubble burst when she began hearing clicks all around them. Frowning, she looked around to see what was going on. "What is that?" Ivy craned her head around Eli, only to gasp when she saw multiple people with their cell phones out, recording and snapping pictures of the two of them walking. "What are they doing?" She felt Eli stiffen under her fingers and glanced up at his face. All emotion had dropped from his features and he had put on a stoic facade. Worried she was upsetting him, Ivy slowly pulled her arm out of his. Ivy had to pick up her pace to keep up with Eli's long legged stride as he sped up, hurrying toward the door of the restaurant.

Once outside, it became even worse.

"Who's the girl, Mr. Truman?" One man shoved a microphone in Eli's face.

"Are you two dating, Mr. Truman?"

"How do you explain your statement only last month that you never planned to date again?"

"Does this woman work with you?"

"What's your name?"

The shouting and flashing lights were overwhelming and Ivy tucked herself behind Eli, burrowing her face in his back. *This is crazy! Is this what Eli goes through all the time?*

Eli had stopped on the sidewalk since they were blocked in from all sides. After trying several times to step through the media without success, he reached behind him to pull Ivy forward.

With a firm grip on her upper arm, Eli held her out to the side. "This is Ms. Ivy Thompson," he said in a loud clear voice. "She works at the Avangarde Castle Resort as a simple, front desk clerk. We were here tonight on a business meeting and nothing more. Now, let us pass or I will call the police."

Eli kept his hold of Ivy as he dragged her through the reluctantly moving crowd. Seeing a familiar face, Ivy looked over and saw the woman who had harassed Eli earlier in the week. Ms. Samuelson stood at the back of the crowd with a smug grin on her face as she watched the media chaos. *Is this her doing?*

Ivy couldn't concentrate enough to say anything to Eli. Tears pricked her eyes as she stumbled after him until they reached his car. *Just a business meeting. Simple front desk clerk. Nothing more.* The words he spoke moments before were burned into her memory.

Numbly, she sat down and buckled her seatbelt as Eli fought his way to the driver's seat. *I will not cry in front of my boss.* Blinking hard and biting her tongue, Ivy held back the flood she knew was waiting.

Eli didn't speak as he drove them back to her apartment. Once he had parked the car, he let out a long breath and laid his head on the steering wheel. "Ivy," he said in a low, tired voice. "Tonight was, obviously, a... a mistake."

No more! Ivy's heart screamed. "Got it," Ivy said brusquely. Quickly, she unbuckled and jumped out of the car. The good manners instilled in her since childhood wouldn't let her leave without saying anything, so she ducked her head back down to the open door. "Thank you for dinner."

Slamming the car door, she ran as fast as she could in her heeled shoes to her apartment door. Once inside, she kicked off her heels and ran for her bed, the tears already streaming down her cheeks.

"Ivy?" Her roommate called out to her as she passed the couch. "Are you okay?"

"I'm fine!" Ivy yelled back as she closed her bedroom door. Once the door was secure, her whole body suddenly felt like a rock. Her limbs and eyes were heavy and tired. She made her way to the bed where she collapsed in a heap of tears and misery.

"Why?" She sniffled into her pillow. "Why let me get a glimpse of something wonderful, only to take it away?" Ivy wanted to pound her pillow, she wanted to rip something to shreds, but she knew it wouldn't do any good.

She had been through this exact emotional upheaval while she took care of her dying mother, and no amount of anger or screaming had changed a thing. All it had done was give her a raging headache and too many sleepless nights. Instead, she curled into her covers and buried her face in her pillow to hide her sobs and soak up her tears.

After crying herself dry, she fell into a restless sleep.

Daylight streamed through Ivy's windows, waking her the next morning. Slowly, she sat up, rubbing her gritty and swollen eyes. She grimaced at the taste left in her mouth and stretched her arms high over her head. *That's what I get for not brushing my teeth last night.* Ivy froze as everything that had occured the night before came back to her.

"Eli..." Ivy mumbled, tears refilling her eyes. "Just a business meeting. A simple, front desk clerk." Putting a hand over her heart, Ivy bent over, as the sharp pain from the night before hit her full force once again.

"How could I have read him so wrong?" Righteous anger began to boil inside of her. She pinched her lips clenched her fists. "I may be a lowly, front desk clerk, but I'm honest and kind and I don't throw people to the wolves." She took a steadying breath. "I've been through heartbreaking things before. I can do it again."

Once inside the bathroom, she turned the water on as hot as she could handle it, using the heat to scrub away everything about the previous night. "No more crush on Mr. Broody, Boss Man. No more offering to go the extra mile and grab him a coffee when he's having a bad day. In fact, no more speaking to him at all if I don't have to. I will be polite but professional." She finished rinsing and stepped out of the tub a new woman.

"I will finish my degree and move somewhere far away where I never have to see his handsome, grouchy face again."

Feeling slightly rebellious, Ivy spent extra time on her makeup and hair. Then took the time to pick out a skirt that showed off her small curves to their best advantage. She couldn't do anything about the button-up shirt she had to wear as part of her uniform, but she threw on her best push-up bra and tucked the shirt in tight.

Feeling confident and strong, she headed into work. "A simple, front desk clerk, my foot."

CHAPTER 9

Eli felt as if the whole world was plotting against him. He groaned as he rubbed his temples with his fingers. "Why me?" He mumbled.

The last seven days had been the worst days of his life. *And it all began with that disastrous date with Ivy.*

When the two of them had been surrounded by the paparazzi, Eli had gone into his normal 'show no emotion' mode. He couldn't hide Ivy, since the crowd had already seen her, so he told them clearly and plainly who she was.

However, when he'd tried to apologize to her for the media, she had left him high and dry. When she'd rushed out of his vehicle, he could see tears trickling down her cheeks and knew she had made her decision. *Obviously, her feelings weren't strong enough to deal with that kind of zoo all the time.*

"And people wonder why I don't want to get remarried," he mumbled.

Seeing her almost every day at work was nearly unbearable. She had shown up the next morning, after their date, bright and fresh as a daisy. She had gone out of her way to help people, charming everyone left and right. Her hair had looked silky and inviting, her makeup done to perfection and the pencil skirts she had taken to wearing, made it hard for Eli to keep his eyes to himself.

And she's talking to everyone... but me. Ivy hadn't spoken a word to Eli since the date. If she had a question, she had started calling Nelson or sending one of the other clerks to ask Eli.

He couldn't blame her. The mess with the media had caught them both off guard. "Just let it go, Eli," he scolded himself. "You learned a long time ago that women aren't worth it. She's obviously doing just fine without you, so just let it go."

"Now that, is a novel idea," Nelson boomed as he burst into Eli's office.

"Not you," Eli groaned, slumping back in his seat.

Nelson gave a crooked grin. "My dear brother, if I didn't know any better, I would think that you aren't happy to see me."

"Well, then obviously, you don't know bettter."

"Ouch! What has you so wound up?" Nelson held up a hand. "Wait, never mind. I saw the news. The woman you are madly in love with isn't speaking to you because you threw her to the wolves and crushed her heart on live television."

Eli jerked upright. "What? You can't be serious." Eli glared at his brother. "First of all, I'm not in love with her. Second, I didn't throw her to the wolves, I was trying to protect her from them."

"Then why isn't she speaking to you?" Nelson raised a cocky eyebrow.

Eli rubbed his temples again. "I don't know. She wouldn't speak to me when I dropped her off, I figured it was because she couldn't handle the paparazzi. Her silence made it clear she wants nothing to do with me." He glared at Nelson. "I didn't plan for that to happen, so there's no way she could blame me for anything."

Nelson scooted his chair forward and leaned his elbows on Eli's desk. "Have you watched the news clip of you two?"

Eli rolled his eyes. "You know I don't watch those stupid things. Why would I encourage something I hate?"

Nelson's face had dropped all traces of humor. "Because maybe you would understand why Ivy was so hurt. You messed up bad, Brother."

Eli opened his mouth to answer, but nothing came out. Finally, he snapped his mouth shut. *Did I really do something wrong? How else was I supposed to handle those man-eaters?*

Nelson slapped his hands on the desk as he stood. "I've got a bunch of openings in a horseback riding excursion tomorrow. It would be better if we had more people. Want to take a break from the stale office and actually feel the sunshine?"

"What?" Eli glanced up from where his eyes had been distractedly boring a hole in his desk. "Uh, yeah, sure, sounds great."

"Sweet! See you at eleven."

Eli nodded but didn't speak. Once Nelson was out of the room, Eli woke up his computer and searched for a clip from last Friday. After a moment of hesitation, he clicked on the video.

Watching himself yank Ivy from behind his back and hold her at arm's length shook him to his core. *The squirt was right. I look like a jerk.* Eli then listened to his little speech about her, watching Ivy's reaction as he spoke. *And I sound even worse. No wonder she hates me.*

He closed the page he had been on. "How did I not see how much that hurt her?" He slumped in his seat. "Ivy deserves so much better."

IVY GLARED AT NELSON. "I'm not falling for that again. Last time I agreed to go have fun with you, you disappeared and left me with your brother."

"Ah, but you had a good time that night, didn't you?" Nelson grinned and pumped his eyebrows up and down.

"That night wasn't bad, but the next one was horrible." Ivy chewed her lip. "Besides, the more I think about it, the more I realize it would never work." She blinked to hold back the prick of tears. "Your brother deserves so much better. He needs a woman who can not only hold her own in front of the media, but one who he is proud to show off."

Nelson rested both elbows on the countertop and leaned in. "Ivy, you're being way too harsh on yourself. Those wolves will chew up anyone and anything. If my brother only needed a woman to look good, he could hire a model to do it. Besides," he straightened up, "it was Eli's fault things went so badly, not yours. Let's put the blame where it belongs."

Ivy barked out a laughed, then quickly covered her mouth. "Now, Nelson, be fair."

"I am and it's totally his fault. In fact, that's why I invited you along for tomorrow, because I felt so bad about what happened last weekend."

Ivy chewed her lip. "Well, horseback riding does sound fun, but I feel funny just joining a group like that. Are you sure it's okay?"

Nelson waved away her concerns like a pesky gnat. "Of course. All the horses need exercise and only a few have actually been hired out tomorrow. It means less work for my crew if we take out a few more."

Ivy narrowed her eyes. "A few more? Who all have you invited?"

"A couple of other workers," Nelson shrugged. "You're not the only one who deserves a little fun now and then."

Ivy relaxed and smiled. "All right, you've convinced me. Thank you for inviting me, Nellie."

A wide smile crossed the handsome man's face. "Great! See you tomorrow at eleven, Fairy Girl."

Ivy gave him a small wave as he strutted away. "Maybe getting out in the sunshine is exactly what I need." She began stacking the pamphlets into neat piles. "Anything to get my mind off Mr. Eli, Jerk, Truman."

CHAPTER 10

I vy walked up to the large barn, put her hands on her hips and took a deep breath. "This is exactly what I need." The sun beat on her back, filling her with warmth and she sighed in contentment.

A few people stood around in circles, chatting as they waited for the workers to bring out the horses.

Ivy adjusted her baseball cap and sunglasses, grateful she had thought to bring them. *I probably should put sunscreen on the back of my neck or I'll be burned to a crisp.* She began rooting around in her backpack for the little bottle she had packed when movement from the side caught her eye.

Glancing up, Ivy stilled. Walking towards her, in all his jean clad glory, was Eli. *I've never seen him out of a suit before.* The closer he got, the more Ivy felt like she might melt. He wore boot-cut, well-worn jeans, with work boots and a tight, graphic t-shirt. *Oh my...* Ivy jerked into movement, afraid that he might see her staring. She touched her bottom lip to be sure she hadn't been drooling before sneaking another glance in his direction.

"Who knew he could fill out clothes like that?" She turned her body and pulled down the brim of her hat, so she could watch him without his noticing. When he waltzed right into the barn, her jaw nearly hit the floor. *Please tell me he's not coming on this ride. Nelson promised it wouldn't be like last time.*

Her frantic wishes were crushed when Eli walked out with Nelson, holding the reins of two horses. *I haven't spent a week avoiding that man just so Nelson can throw us back together.*

Nelson stood at the front of the barn and began giving his usual speech about safety and following directions. Ivy didn't hear a word he said, her mind was too busy trying to figure out how to get away from the situation without anyone noticing.

Once the talk was over, Nelson smiled wide and began calling out names and helping people onto their horses.

Now's my chance. Ivy slowly turned and took a couple of steps, determined to get away.

"Ivy?" Nelson's amused voice rang out over the group and Ivy paused. "I've got Poppycock all ready for you."

Ivy turned back, glaring at Nelson with icy daggers. However, the grin on his face attested to the fact that he knew exactly what she had been trying to do. *Keep grinning, Buddy. If I took off my sunglasses, I'd melt you into a puddle.*

With stiff movements, she worked her way over to where he stood. From the corner of her eye, she could see Eli helping another woman on to her horse. His movements were just as jerky as hers. *Guess he didn't know I was coming either.*

When she got to the horse, she paused with her foot in the stirrup. "You are a dead man, Nellie" she whispered before stepping up into the saddle.

Nelson smirked. "You'll thank me, later," he returned cockily.

Ivy rolled her eyes, but once again her sunglasses hid her reaction. As she began to turn the horse so they could step out of the way, Eli grabbed Nelson's arm and pulled him over to the other side of the barn. Ivy watched as a heated exchange took place.

Pain pricked her chest, and it became difficult to breathe. *Does he hate me that much? I mean, he made it clear I wasn't good enough for him, but now I can't even join in the activities around the resort?*

"Who does he think he is?" She muttered quietly.

"Oh, that's Mr. Truman, he owns the resort," a feminine voice interrupted Ivy's tirade.

"I know- uh, thank you," Ivy muttered as she looked over at the woman. *Figures.* Ivy pinched her lips to keep from frowning. The woman next to her was dressed to the nines in cowgirl gear. It was obvious the woman had money, just as it was equally obvious her outfit was brand new.

The tall, cool beauty leaned toward Ivy. "Rumor has it he doesn't date. But just last week he was seen taking a woman to dinner." She straightened and sniffed. "She turned out to be someone who worked for him, so it wasn't like anything was going on, but that little evening opens the door perfectly for someone like me."

Ivy's eyebrows shot up. "Someone like you?"

"Well, of course, Honey. A front desk clerk certainly isn't worthy of a man like Eli Truman," she fluffed her hair, "but I am. I come from wealth and know exactly how to handle a man and lifestyle like that."

"I'll just bet you do," Ivy muttered. It was obvious the woman hadn't recognized Ivy as the 'someone who worked for him' from the video. *Probably best to keep it that way.* "Excuse me," Ivy took her horse and turned her toward the outer rim of the group, determined not to talk any more of the guests. Today's relaxing outing just became a nightmare.

Planting herself and her horse just outside the main group, Ivy waited, albeit restlessly, for things to get underway.

Eventually, Nelson slapped a scowling Eli on the back and they headed toward their horses. Once they were mounted, Nelson took his horse to the front of the group. "We're going to keep a nice easy pace, I will lead in the front and my brother Eli will bring up the rear. Please stay in between the two of us. If you're having trouble with your horse, make sure to flag one of use down. Otherwise, enjoy the ride and the scenery." He turned his horse toward the rolling hills. "Giddy-yap, cowboy!" Nelson waved his straw cowboy hat in the air, making the group laugh, and started the train of horses.

Shoot. Ivy bit her lip. *Now what?* She had planned to stick to the back of the group so she didn't have to converse with anyone. *Especially*

Nelson or Eli. But with one in the front and one in the back, her options were limited.

She studied the group for a minute trying to figure out her best choice. When she saw Ms. Wealthy turn her horse so she could ride beside Eli, Ivy knew the decision had been made for her. With her stomach churning in despair and jealousy, Ivy kicked her horse toward the front of the group. *Even Nelson would be better than being stuck in the middle.*

The group rode for a while in relative silence. There were small murmurs as individuals chatted to those close to them, but for the most part things were peaceful.

Maybe this won't be so bad. Ivy let herself relax and enjoy the lush, green landscape of the Pacific Northwest. Closing her eyes for a moment, Ivy tilted her head back and let the sun's rays warm her cheeks. Being on the eastern side of the state meant they got a lot of rain, but today's weather was a welcome reprieve from their normally gray skies.

"I'm just guessing here, but with skin like yours, I'm thinking you'll either end up bright red or with a million freckles by the end of the day." Nelson sounded like he was holding in laughter as he broke into Ivy's peace.

"I've never gotten freckles and I have on sunscreen, so there," Ivy retorted without opening her eyes. Between the warmth of the sun and the consistent, comfortable shifting of the horse beneath her, Ivy knew if she wasn't careful she would nod off. Reluctantly, she opened her eyes and looked over at Nelson, who was smirking.

"Thought you might be sleeping there for a minute," he teased.

"If I wasn't concerned about falling off, I might have taken a nap." She sighed dramatically. "I'm afraid I'm not enough of a horsewoman to sleep in the saddle."

"Eh, we'll fix that soon enough."

Ivy straightened and glared at her friend. "Oh, no you don't. This is the second time I've fallen for your lies. If you think I will ever do anything with you ever again, you're sadly mistaken."

Nelson's eyes widened. "What in the world are you talking about? I've never lied to you!"

Ivy tilted her head to the side, pursed her lips and glared. "Oh really? What about the night you asked me to dinner?"

"Did you or did you not get a free dinner out of the evening?"

"I did, but you-"

"And I even paid for it." He grinned. "Eli brought me the bill, so I didn't lie about anything. I bought you dinner just like I said I would."

Ivy rolled her eyes. "All right, what about today?"

Nelson shrugged and led his horse around a large rock in the road. "What about today?"

"You specifically didn't tell me that Eli was coming."

"Ah, but I didn't lie. I said other workers were coming, and they did." Nelson grinned again.

Ivy pointed a finger at him. "You knew I wouldn't come if Eli was coming so you didn't tell me he was coming. It was a lie by omission."

Nelson scowled. "How can I lie by not saying something? If I didn't say it, I didn't lie about it."

"You made me think-"

"Don't put this on me, Ivy. You're the one who inferred Eli wasn't one of the workers who was coming. No one made you think that but yourself."

"He's not a worker, he's an owner." Ivy pointed out.

"Who works here, so he is, in fact, a worker. You didn't ask for the names of the workers." Nelson shook his head. "Admit it, I didn't lie, you just didn't do your research."

"You are the most exasperating man, Nellie Truman."

"Only you can get away with calling me that, Fairy Girl," Nelson muttered with a frown.

Ivy laughed, glad she had finally gotten in a shot. Nelson hated the nickname 'Nellie' but since their relationship was more like a brother/sister bond, she got away with it where others didn't.

Nelson suddenly straightened and began frantically patting his saddle bags.

"What's the matter?" Ivy asked, the edges of her mouth turning down.

"I think I forgot the first aid kit," Nelson said as he began digging through his stuff.

"Is someone hurt?" Ivy looked around, not seeing anything amiss. Her eyes landed on the rich girl she had spoken to earlier. She noted with satisfaction that the woman was not riding beside Eli any longer. *Knock it off, Ivy. He's not yours and you're better than that.*

"No, no one's hurt, but by law I have to have one with me." Nelson sighed as he took his hat off and ran his hands through his hair. "We're going to have to turn back."

Ivy's eyebrows shot up. "The whole group? We've already been traveling for forty-five minutes. If you turn us around there won't be enough time for these folks to get their ride in."

Nelson scrunched his lips to one side. "I guess I'll have to give a bunch of refunds then, but if someone does get hurt and I don't have anything to help, it could mean a lawsuit."

Ivy's heart sank. "No, don't do that. I'll run back and get it. By myself, I can pick up the pace and meet back up with you in no time."

Nelson studied her. "Are you sure? That would ruin the nice, relaxing time I promised you."

Ivy shrugged. "Watching other girls flirt with Eli isn't exactly relaxing, anyway." Ivy gasped and put her hand of her mouth. "Oooh," she groaned. "One of these days I'm going to have to put duct tape on my mouth.

Nelson threw his head back and laughed. "If you think I don't know how you feel about my brother, then you are sorely mistaken,

Fairy Girl. It's more than obvious to anyone who pays attention that you're gone on him."

"Are you serious?" Ivy whispered harshly as she leaned forward. "Does the whole resort know I have a crush on him?"

"Nah, I know because, contrary to popular opinion, I actually pay attention to what's going on around me. As far as I know, nobody else has said anything about it."

Ivy's shoulder fell. "Although, I guess I'm just one of dozens, huh? So it probably doesn't matter if anyone else knows."

Nelson sent her a sharp look. "No pity parties, Ivy. You're not just one of the crowd and you know it. Eli likes you just as much as you like him, he's just too stubborn to admit it."

Ivy shook her head. "He made it clear how he felt last week, Nellie," she said softly. Before Nelson could respond, she sat up straighter. "Anyway, enough. Like you said, no pity parties. I'll run grab that kit and be back as quick as I can."

Nelson's lips were pressed into a thin, white line, but he let the subject drop. "All right. Look, if you go back a few minutes and take the trail next to that huge clump of evergreens, it will save you twenty minutes."

Ivy nodded, tuned her horse around and worked her way to the back of the group. She was aware of Eli's eyes on her as she passed him, but she refused to make eye contact. Once she was clear of the group, she kicked Poppycock into a trot and kept her eyes peeled for the trail Nelson mentioned.

ELI WATCHED IVY HEAD back toward the resort with narrowed eyes. *What is she doing?* He glanced over his shoulder and saw her begin to trot once she was away from the group. With a growl, he picked his way through the other riders to Nelson.

Nelson. He wanted to strangle his brother. Eli had no doubt that Nelson had purposefully brought both he and Ivy on the trip to try to get them to talk to each other. On one hand, Eli did want to apologize to Ivy. On the other, he wanted Nelson to butt out of his business.

While Eli had been riding in the back, he had watched Nelson and Ivy chatting. The way she smiled and bantered with his brother made him want to hit something. *She's not yours, idiot. And never will be, no matter how attracted to her you are.*

"What happened?" Eli asked curtly as he caught up to Nelson.

Nelson turned from the girl he was flirting with a wide smile on his face. "Oh, hey Eli. What's up?"

Eli fought to hold on to a calm exterior. "What happened to Ivy? Why did she head back?"

Nelson shrugged. "I don't know. Said she forgot something." He scrunched his nose. "I probably should have checked to make sure she knew the trail well before letting her go. I mean, she's been on the ride before, but most girls don't have the best sense of direction do they?" He chuckled.

Eli grit his teeth. "Are you saying you just let her go without any instructions? How could you do that?"

Nelson frowned. "No need to get all worked up. I'm sure she'll be fine. She's normally pretty intelligent."

"Pretty intelli-! Nelson, sometimes I wonder how the heck we can be brothers." Eli shook his head. "Go back to your flirting, I'm going to go find her."

Before Nelson could respond, Eli spun his horse around and took off in the same direction as Ivy.

Pushing his horse to a gallop, he caught sight of her trotting along over the next rise. As he was watching, she turned off the trail and disappeared behind a heavy group of trees.

"What is she doing?" He growled. Despite the fact that he was pushing his horse, it seemed to take forever for him to reach the side trail she had taken. "This is barely a path," he grumbled as he dodged tree branches and rocks. He had to slow down his horse in order to navigate the terrain.

"Ivy!" Eli shouted, trying to get a better feel for how far she was in front of him.

When no one answered, he began to worry he would never catch up to her. "Ivy!" He bellowed.

A short scream caught his attention, along with the pounding of hooves. Fear gripped Eli in the chest and he picked up the pace of his horse as fast as he dared. Coming around a corner, he spotted Ivy on the ground, crushing a mound of wildflowers.

"Ivy!" Panic took over his actions as he jumped from his horse and darted to her side. "What happened, are you all right?" Eli looked her over from head to toe, brushing his arms over her limbs in an attempt to check for any breaks.

After a moment, Ivy seemed to have caught her breath, and she glared at Eli. "I'm fine, no thanks to you, you big oaf!" Ivy shoved Eli's hands away from her and tried to stand. "Ooh," she grabbed her head and stumbled.

Without thinking about it, Eli immediately swept the petite woman into his arms and strode over to a fallen log. Gently, he set her down before squatting in front of her. "What's wrong? Is it your head?"

Ivy sat stiff as a board as Eli lifted her cap off her head and gently began running his fingers through her hair. His worry overrode every other sensation, including the feel of her soft silky hair against his fingertips.

"Ouch!" She winced when he touched a bump on the side of her head.

"Hang on, I need to see how bad it is," Eli murmured, his eyes intent on the spot. He pulled out her braid and separated her hair. "Looks like you've got a pretty, good goose egg." He touched it again and sent Ivy an apologetic look when she grimaced.

Ivy waved him off. "I'm sure I'll be fine, thank you." Again she tried to stand and again she nearly fell when a dizzy spell ran through her.

"How about you just have a seat and rest for a bit?" Eli gripped her upper arms and guided her back down. *Stubborn woman, just wait for a few minutes.*

"This is all your fault," she scolded, putting her head in her hands.

Eli jerked back. "What do you mean this is my fault? I'm here to help you.".

"If you hadn't shouted my name and surprised me, I wouldn't have jerked on my horse, who obviously took umbrage to the situation and kicked me off before bolting."

Eli frowned. "You fell because I called your name?"

Ivy turned her head sideways, "It would seem that way, wouldn't it?"

Nothing but the sounds of birds could be heard for the next few minutes.

Eli's jaw clenched, and he felt his teeth grinding as he tried to hold in his anger. For months he had been stuffing his attraction and frustrations in a box and it was getting harder and harder to keep the lid closed. Words were on the tip of his tongue that he knew he shouldn't say, but her anger fed his own and they soon spilled from his mouth. "Well, if you hadn't run off the trail, I wouldn't have chased after you."

Ivy jerked her head up, winced, then focused her glare at him. "So, now this is my fault? I didn't ask you to come racing after me. I would have been just fine if you had stayed with the group."

"You know, Nelson told me you were fairly intelligent, but after sitting here listening to you blame me for your problems, I have to say I disagree with his assessment." *Maybe if I keep her angry, it'll quell this attraction between us.*

Fire flashed in Ivy's eyes and her lips thinned. "Well, it's good to know what you really think. As if you didn't already make it clear last week when you introduced me to the media." Ivy jumped to her feet, only to close her eyes and put her hand to her head before straightening and storming off in the direction her horse had left.

"I suppose you want me to help you find your horse," Eli grumbled as he stood up and brushed dirt off of his seat. Her words had hit too close to home and some of his anger ebbed away. *She's right. I was a total jerk last week.*

"No, thank you. I think you've done enough." Ivy said over her shoulder.

Eli shook his head as guilt ate at his core. "Come on, Ivy." He ran his fingers through his hair in frustration. "Let me help you."

"I said no!"

By now, Ivy was out of sight. *She's going to get lost and then I'll be in even more trouble.* Eli growled, grabbed the reins of his horse, and stomped after her into the woods. For several minutes nobody spoke as they made their way through the foliage trying to find signs of Poppycock.

After fifteen minutes of searching, Ivy threw her hands up in the air and let out a huff. "Where the heck could he be?"

"My guess is he's halfway back to the barn by now," Eli muttered looking around the dense forest.

Ivy spun around frowning. "Are you serious? Why didn't you say so before?"

Eli raised and eyebrow. "You've made it pretty clear you don't want to hear what I have to say. You seem to be under the impression that I'm always wrong."

Ivy rolled her eyes and flopped down on the ground, muttering something about men. After a moment, she raised her head, "Look, this isn't getting us anywhere. Can we call a truce? At least until we get back to the resort?"

Eli felt his shoulders slump as most of the tension drained out of them. With a nod, he walked over and sat down next to Ivy. "I'm sorry," he said quietly.

Ivy sat up and studied the man beside her. "It's okay. I'm also sorry that I snapped at you."

Eli shook his head and rubbed his hands over his face. "No. I'm sorry for everything."

"Everything?" Ivy squeaked. "What exactly do you mean, everything?"

"I'm sorry for how I've brushed you off all these months at the resort, I'm sorry for how I acted at the end of our date, especially what I said to the media, I'm sorry I didn't clarify things between us after that." He took a fortifying breath. "And I'm especially sorry I chased after you and caused you to have an accident."

Eli played with the fallen pine needles at his feet and gave a self-deprecating laugh. "Funny thing is, I thought I was doing the right thing all this time." He ran a hand over his ball cap. "By staying away from you at work, I thought my attraction to you would go away. After all, why would a gorgeous, innocent, young thing like you be interested in a grizzled, old bear like myself?"

Ivy's eyes widened and her breathing quickened.

"And then at dinner the other night, I thought if I told the media about your job, they would let the matter drop, assuming our evening was work related. I figured they would leave you alone." He let out a soft growl. "I didn't want them hounding you the way they've hounded me and my brothers."

Eli glanced over at Ivy and his eyes widened. "Breathe, Ivy," he commanded, grabbing her shoulders.

All color had drained from Ivy's face. Her mouth hung open and in her shock, she had frozen. With a sudden gasp, she blinked rapidly and started sucking in oxygen.

Eli's grip softened, and he began running his hands up and down her arms. "I never meant to hurt you. Nelson took me to task and forced me to watch that stupid video of us outside the restaurant." He hung his head and blew out a big breath. "It wasn't until I watched it from another perspective that I realized how it must have sounded to you. When you ran off after our date, I just assumed you were upset about the mob and wanted nothing to do with me." Eli looked up and grimaced. "I usually don't mess things up so badly."

Ivy's eyes warmed at his words. "Don't apologize very often, huh?"

Eli chuckled and shook his head. Unable to resist the temptation any longer, he raised a knuckle and rubbed it along her soft, flushed cheek.

Reaching up, she put her hand over his, flattening his palm against her skin. "Thank you, Eli. And of course I can forgive you, but can you forgive me?"

Eli's momentary smiled quickly plummeted into a frown. He put both hands up to bracket her face. "What in the world do you need forgiving for?"

Ivy's eyes dropped to the ground. "After our dinner, I thought you were telling everyone how I wasn't good enough for you. I may have thought some really nasty things about you. Then, I proceeded to ignore you all week. It probably wasn't the most mature way to handle the situation and I'm sorry." She kept her eyes down and nibbled on her lip.

"Let me get this straight," Eli gave a slight pull to force Ivy to bring her eyes up. "You want me to forgive you for having bad thoughts about me?"

"Well, yeah. And for ignoring you."

Eli closed his eyes and brought his forehead to rest on hers. "Ivy, you are by far the most tender hearted woman I have ever met." He chuckled lightly and gave a light kiss to her forehead. "There's nothing to forgive, Sweetheart."

"Wow," she breathed. "I need to think bad thoughts about you more often." She bit her lip again, this time to hold back a smile.

"You keep biting that lip and I'm going to need to ask forgiveness again," Eli murmured. He rubbed his nose down the side of her face, working his way closer to her lips. *How does she smell so good after sitting on a horse for the last hour? Will she let me kiss her?* She wasn't moving away from his touch, so, cautiously, tenderly, Eli brushed his lips against hers. *Holy cow...* He felt as if he had been struck by lightning from their small touch. But as much as he wanted to pull her in close and experience more of their magic, he forced himself to pull back just enough to see her reaction.

"Oh, no, you don't," Ivy grabbed his face and pulled him back down to her mouth.

Eli chuckled against her lips only for a moment before getting down to serious business. It felt as if she had been made just for him. Her lips were just as delectable as he thought they would be and he took full advantage.

Letting go of her face, he ran his hands down her back and pulled her in as close as they could get sitting side by side on the ground.

Ivy's hands wandered up and wrapped around his neck. When she bumped into his baseball cap, she flicked it to the ground, unwilling to let it get in the way of her exploration.

"I've got hat hair," Eli murmured against her skin as he kissed across her jaw line.

"I don't care," Ivy said as she turned and brought him back to her lips.

Seconds turned into minutes and minutes turned into lost time as they continued to hold each other. A loud snort and a shove nearly knocked Eli flat on the ground and finally broke the bubble Ivy and he had wrapped themselves in.

"All right, all right," Eli said, shoving his horse's face away from the two of them. "You're right, we should get back."

Stupid horse. Eli scowled at the creature for a moment. *Do you have any idea how long I've waited to do something like that?*

With a sigh, Ivy stood up and brushed off her seat.

Eli followed suit, then grabbed both of their hats from off the ground. After slapping his on his head, he reached up to put on Ivy's. "Your cheeks are pink." He ran a finger down one. "I should have left your hat on so you wouldn't get sunburned."

"I'm pretty sure my entire body is on fire from those kisses, so who knows how much of it is from the sun." Ivy paused as soon as the words left her mouth. Closing her eyes, she groaned.

Feeling lighter than he had in years, Eli laughed lightly and wrapped Ivy up in his arms, kissing the top of her head. "I have a feeling life is never dull with you, Fairy Girl."

"Not you too!" Ivy pulled back so she could tie off her braid, then grabbed her hat from Eli. "Nelson only calls me that to annoy me." She pursed her lips and tilted her head from side to side. "And because I call him Nellie." One side of her mouth quirked in a grin.

"Nellie?" Eli threw his head back and laughed loud and long.

Ivy looked mesmerized as she watched him wipe tears from his eyes.

"I'm so going to have to start calling him that." Eli took a deep breath. "Or maybe, I'll just tell Hayden and let him handle it." Eli shook his head.

Ivy huffed and crossed her arms over her chest. "That still doesn't give you permission to call me Fairy Girl."

Eli's smile was wide as he stepped forward and put his face next to hers. "And what would you like me to call you?"

Ivy rolled her eyes. "Well, my name is always pleasant. Or you could, you know, say something romantic like, oh, I don't know, sweetheart, darling, most wonderful person I've ever met..." Ivy raised her eyebrows and made little circles with her hand, encouraging him to continue.

Eli chuckled again as he pulled her in close, nuzzling her neck. "I'll see what I can come up with," he murmured.

"See that you do," Ivy whispered back.

Eli pulled back, immediately missing her softness, but knowing they needed to get going. "So, what exactly did you need to go back for?" He gathered the reins of his horse.

"Nelson sent me back to grab the first aid kit. He said if someone got hurt he could get sued if he didn't have it."

Eli froze. "The first aid kit? Are you serious?"

Ivy's back had been to Eli. She turned around and frowned. "Well, yeah. He said he forgot it and when I volunteered to grab it for him, he said to take the short-cut."

Eli closed his eyes and banged his head on the saddle. "I'm gonna kill him," he grumbled.

Ivy walked over and tentatively put her hand on Eli's shoulder. "What's the matter?"

He raised his head. "We've been had. Again," he stated with a scowl. "Nelson set us up."

Ivy fisted her hands on her hips. "How exactly did he manage it this time?"

"By lying." Eli sighed. "Although he does carry a first aid kit on these rides, it has never left his saddle bag. There is no way he doesn't have it. Not only does he check things, but so do both of the barn workers. So it was triple checked before we came. Not to mention, this isn't a short-cut," he waved his arm around the area. "It's barely even a trail. He knew if you took it, you would get lost. He also knew that you taking off would make me concerned. When I asked him where you were going he said you had forgotten something and wanted to go back. He's just lucky I saw you take this turnoff," Eli growled out the last bit.

"So, I could have been stuck out here?"

"No, I would have found you, and if all else failed, your horse would have brought you home, but it might have taken a while. Not to mention it would have taken ten years off my life."

Ivy smiled coyly and stepped into Eli's space. Slowly, she slid her arms up his arms and around his shoulders. "You would have come for me?"

"Sweetheart, I did come for you," Eli grinned and kissed her nose.

"But I wasn't lost."

"Well, not now you're not."

"Who are you and what did you do with my grumpy boss?" Ivy grinned.

"Knowing me, I'm sure he'll be back, but right now, he's taking a break." Eli leaned in, closing the distance between him and Ivy.

"Be sure to let him know I'm on break too," Ivy murmured right before Eli took over the conversation.

After a few minutes, Eli reluctantly pulled back. "We need to get back to the resort," he murmured softly, then leaned in to kiss Ivy's cheek.

"I know," Ivy sighed, burying her face in his neck. Neither wanted to leave their little forest haven and go back to the real world, but both knew the return was inevitable. "What does all this mean?" Ivy said softly.

Eli frowned and pulled back. "What does what mean?"

Ivy straightened and stepped out of his embrace. "This." She waved a hand between the two of them. "This kissing and holding and you admitting your feelings Where does this put us?"

"Does it really have to put us anywhere? You know I'm attracted to you and from your response I would say you feel the same for me. Does it have to mean something beyond that?"

Ivy jerked back as if she had been slapped.

Eli held in a grimace *Surely, after all we've talked about, she understands that we can't really go anywhere. I made that clear before.*

"So... are you saying you want to be friends?" Ivy's voice was calm, too calm, and it put Eli on his guard.

"Yes," he said cautiously.

"Do you kiss all your friends like this?"

"No."

"So, what? You want to be friends with benefits?"

Eli rubbed his face. "It sounds bad when you say it like that. But after everything I've told you, I would think you would understand why this can't work."

"Why what can't work? Us?"

Eli shrugged and nodded. "Well, yeah. I told you after my divorce I decided I was done. And you saw the media frenzy the other night. That would be going on twenty-four-seven if we were together. They would hound you at your apartment and neither of us would ever get any peace. There's no way we can start anything other than maybe a casual relationship. You have to be able to see that," he pleaded.

"Casual." Ivy's voice had dropped even further and her eyes began to look misty.

Now, you've done it. This is exactly why it's better to stay away. I should have never kissed her. But a loud part of his brain couldn't feel bad about their encounter. Never before had a woman felt so right, so good in his arms, and there was no true way to regret finding that miracle.

Ivy's lips firmed and she straightened her spine. "I'm sorry, Mr. Truman. Today was quite obviously a mistake. I got caught up in-the-moment and lost my good sense. It won't happen again." She turned and began marching through the foliage.

What? "Wait! Where are you going?"

"Home!" Ivy shouted without stopping.

Eli grabbed the reins of his horse and caught up to her. "Here, we can ride together."

"No, thank you." Ivy kept her chin up and continued pushing forward.

Stubborn woman. "I mean it, Ivy, it's several miles to the resort."

"Great. It will give me a chance to clear my head. You go on ahead." She kept her eyes forward, refusing to look at him and Eli felt his anger begin to simmer.

"Ivy." He pulled on her arm until she stopped and looked at him. Her bright green eyes blazed with fire and Eli swallowed hard. "Stop being so stubborn and let me get you home."

"Stubborn? Me? Really?" Ivy's jaw dropped, and she scoffed. "Ha! You don't know the meaning of the word! Of the two of us, you are by far the most stubborn." Her eyebrows slashed down, and she took an angry step in his direction, poking him in the chest with her finger. "You are so caught up in the stupid actions of one woman that you've shut yourself off for life from anything good."

"Hey!" Eli glared at her, but she cut him off.

"Understand this, Mr. Truman. I'm not looking for a casual relationship. I don't hand out my affection to any good-looking male who happens to cross my path. I will be saving my kisses for a man who actually wants to be with me, thank you very much. One who doesn't feel the need to hide me from other people. One who doesn't care that I'm just a lowly front desk clerk. I see no point in entering a relationship that we know won't go anywhere. So you can just take your grouchy, stubborn self and stuff it!" She spun around and began walking again, her fists clenched at her sides.

Eli stood still, his jaw gaping, as she marched away from him. His mind was completely blank and words failed him at her tirade. When she finally disappeared from view, he was shaken from his stupor. "Fine," he muttered to himself, walking after her. "If she doesn't want what I'm willing to give, that's just fine. We can go right back to just boss and employee, exactly how it should be." *Then why does this feel so wrong?*

Eli didn't say another word as he followed Ivy back to the resort. *I have a responsibility to make sure she gets back safely.* He reminded himself whenever he was tempted to jump on his mount and leave her in the dust. Their progress was slow, and the sun had begun to wane by the time they got back.

When Ivy veered toward the parking lot, Eli shook his head and continued on toward the barn. After making sure Poppycock had arrived safely, he handed his own horse off to one of the workers and stalked across the grounds to his house.

CHAPTER 11

A month later, Eli's mood hadn't improved. He sunk deeper and deeper into his cold persona, shutting out everyone and everything.

On the weekends and evenings he locked himself in his cabin and refused to speak to anyone from the outside world. Inside, he ached for the warmth and rightness that Ivy had brought into his life, but on the outside, he spoke and acted like the heartless jerk the media made him out to be.

As he slumped on his couch one evening, watching yet another home improvement rerun, he ran his hand through his hair, gripping it tightly. "Why can't she see that it won't work? No matter how attracted we are to each other."

He jumped up and stomped to his kitchen for a cup of water. Gulping down the whole thing, he slammed it down on the counter, breaking the glass.

Eli cursed, then stepped back to grab his broom out of the pantry. "Perfect. This is just... perfect," he muttered as he cleaned up the mess.

"What did you do?"

Eli froze in his crouched position and closed his eyes. *What else can go wrong?* Standing up, Eli turned to face his brothers. "What do you want?" He sneered at Nelson.

Nelson raised an eyebrow. "Testy, are we?"

Eli glared. "You have no idea."

"Why aren't you answering your phone? Or your door for that matter?" Hayden leaned his thick shoulder against the doorframe and folded his arms over his chest.

"Because I wanted to be alone!" Eli threw the glass shards in the garbage and chucked the broom into the pantry. "Is that so hard to believe?"

Nelson pursed his lips and tipped his head from side to side. "Kinda. I mean, usually you're business twenty-four-seven, so..."

"Well, maybe I'm trying not to work so hard." Eli stormed past them and laid down on the couch.

His brothers followed and Eli wondered how they would react if he stood up and physically kicked them out the door.

"I think it's time we had a little chat," Nelson started, throwing his leg over his knee.

"Go ahead, but don't expect me to participate," Eli retorted.

"We've allowed you to not participate for a month, Eli. Now shut up and listen up." Hayden said with a scowl.

Eli jerked upright. "You have no right-"

"We have every right!" Hayden shouted right back. He leaned forward in his chair and pointed at Eli. "You have been moping around for a month and not only are we your brothers, but your behavior is starting to affect the business."

"The business." Eli fell back against the cushions. "Everybody already knows I'm the Ice King."

"No, everybody thought you were firm but fair. Now, you're a brooding idiot." Nelson folded his arms and narrowed his gaze. "You know, I've looked up to you my whole life. You always seemed to have it together. Even when that witch you married took off. You stayed calm, collected and kept moving forward. But now," Nelson shook his head, "now I don't even recognize you. How can you live like this? Would it really be that bad to let another woman into your life?"

Eli stood and began to pace. "Yes. No." He put his hands on his head. "I don't know."

"What's the big deal? Ivy is as sweet as sugar." Hayden grimaced. "Actually, a little too sweet for my tastes, but I guess we're not talking about me. Why are you so scared of a relationship with her?"

Eli stopped pacing and faced his brother. "Who says I'm scared?"

Nelson and Hayden looked at each other and burst out laughing.

"Everything about your actions says you are scared, Big Bro," Hayden said as he wiped his eyes.

Eli pointed his finger back and forth between his guests. "You just wait until this happens to you. Everything about women makes a man lose his head."

Nelson continued to chuckle, but Hayden got suspiciously quiet.

Eli narrowed his eyes, but didn't comment. With a groan, he flopped back down on the couch. "So, what do I do? We didn't part on good terms, no matter how much she puts on a smile for work."

Nelson shrugged. "It's easy. You just have to tell her what an idiot you've been." He put one hand out to the side. "She forgives you," he put out the other hand, "you stop being a sissy and BAM!" He slapped his hands together. "Everything is hunky dory."

Hayden rolled his eyes. "Nelson, you're a bigger idiot than Eli."

"Oh, yeah? Where's your big idea? Chicks dig it when a man grovels." He jerked his chin up. "Makes them feel in charge." He nodded sagely.

Eli stared at Nelson with an expression of disbelief on his face. "You can't be serious. Where the heck do you get your ideas from? Have you been reading Teen Magazine again?"

Nelson looked affronted while Hayden snickered. "What do you mean again? When have I ever read teenage girl magazines?"

"There was that one time-"

"Oh, shut up, Hayden. Your idea of romance is to show her how to poach an egg."

Hayden growled and folded his arms. "It's harder than you think. Most people completely overcook them."

Eli's head was bouncing back and forth between his brothers. "Are you kidding me right now?" He finally burst in. "We're talking about me and Ivy, not your favorite breakfast foods."

"So, are you finally ready to ask her out for real this time? No more yanking her chain?" Nelson raised an eyebrow.

"I wasn't trying to yank her chain to begin with!" Eli threw up his arms. "I told her up front we couldn't be together."

"And yet you still took her to dinner." Hayden pointed out.

"Only as a cover story for that blogger lady."

"But then you went after her on the horse ride." Nelson tilted his head.

"Because you set us up," Eli retorted.

"Still, you've been sending mixed signals." Nelson shrugged.

Eli slumped. "You're right."

"Dude!" Nelson's face lit up. "I should get that in writing!"

"Get out," Eli said, amusement in his tone. "We're done here."

"But I didn't get-"

"Come on, Squirt." Hayden grabbed Nelson's shirt collar and pulled him toward the doorway. "Our work here is done."

"Next time, I'm gonna use a voice recorder!" Nelson shouted as he walked out.

Hayden paused in the doorway and looked over his shoulder. "Despite the fact that I think you and Ivy are perfect for each other, I want you to know that we'll support whichever way you choose to go. But I have to tell ya, you need to man up. Either give this thing a chance or completely let go. What you're doing now isn't helping anybody."

Eli nodded, all traces of amusement gone. "Got it."

Hayden nodded and pulled the door closed behind him.

The silence that followed their departure was almost overwhelming. Eli stood and began to pace again. "Okay, let's look at this logically. Why do I want Ivy?" He paused. "Well, she's gorgeous, that's easy." He took a few more steps. He pictured her in his mind. Her bright smile and big, green eyes. He thought of watching her work at the resort and how she interacted with the people around her. They always left her presence with a smile on their faces, almost like they couldn't help it. Her sunny personality was infectious.

He sat on the ottoman; leaning forward on his knees. "But it's more than that. She's kind, intelligent, hard working. She treats everyone with respect." He thought of how he had been so cold to her. "Even when they don't deserve it." His voice dropped. "But is it worth the possible heartache?" He put his face in his hands. For the first time in many weeks, he let himself think back to their kiss in the forest. For a few moments, all had been right in the world. His broken parts had finally felt whole.

"Yeah... it's worth it. Anything is better than how I'm feeling now." He straightened his back and put his hand on his knees. "But I've screwed up twice now. How am I going to get her to give me another chance?" Grimacing, Eli pulled out his phone and did something he never thought he would do. He texted Nelson.

Can you help me win her back?

Aha! I got it in writing this time! I'm totally taking a screenshot of this for future blackmail.

Eli groaned and sunk back into his couch. *I better not regret this. What am I saying? I already regret it.* He sighed.

Are you going to answer the question or not?

I'm on it! Just leave it to me. ;)

"Ah, crap," Eli muttered. "What have I gotten myself into?"

IVY FELT LIKE SHE WAS dying. For a month straight, she had smiled, cajoled, teased, served and done her job with a smile on her face. For a month straight, she had pretended that her boss hadn't broken her heart. She had tried to convince herself that everything was as it should be, that it was better to let him go, that her feelings for him were simply a result of his handsome face, but nothing worked.

Each day, she broke a little more, and she wasn't sure how much longer she could keep going. A night hadn't gone by that she hadn't relived the kiss she and Eli had shared, but it was inevitably followed by a few tears when she remembered that she wasn't enough for him.

She had eaten more ice cream than any one person should ever consume and if she wasn't careful, she wasn't going to be able to fit into her swimsuit next summer.

Heidi, her roommate had encouraged her to look for other jobs and Ivy had to admit to herself that she was considering the idea. *Or maybe I'll just take out that loan I've been putting off and go to school full-time.*

She sighed as she carried a stack of towels toward the indoor pool attached to the far side of the castle. "I don't want to go into more debt, but if he doesn't lighten up, I might not have a choice," she grumbled.

Pasting a smile on her face, Ivy walked into the humid room and restocked the towel rack. She smiled and waved at the little children splashing and wished her life was just as carefree.

"Did you miss me?" Ivy teased when she got back to the front desk.

Janet grinned at her. "Of course! I always miss your smile when you're not around." She glanced around and leaned over; lowering her voice. "And apparently, I'm not the only one."

Ivy frowned. "What's that supposed to mean?"

Janet winked. "Nelson was here looking for you."

Ivy rolled her eyes. "Nelson and I are just friends. He's like a brother to me."

Janet pursed her lips and nodded. "Mm hm, that's what they all say."

Ivy laughed. "Seriously, Janet. We're just friends." Ivy began folding maps. "Did Nelson say what he wanted?"

Janet shook her head. "Nah, said he would catch up to you later."

Ivy nodded. "Thanks."

Several hours later, Ivy sighed as she clocked out and headed toward the side door of the castle. *I'm exhausted. Tonight is definitely a hot bath night.*

"Wassup, Ives?" Nelson's booming voice jolted Ivy, and she spun with her hand on her heart.

"Nellie! You nearly gave me a heart attack!" Bending over and putting her hands on her knees, Ivy took slow, deep breaths to calm her pulse back down.

"Oops," Nelson said with a mischievous grin. "Sorry."

Ivy stood and slugged him in the shoulder. "Yeah, yeah, I can tell you really feel bad."

Nelson laughed. "How about I make it up to you?"

Ivy eyed him warily. "By doing what?"

Nelson narrowed his eyes and tapped his lips. "How about dinner?"

Ivy sent a deadpan look his way. "I think we've done that before and we both know how it turned out." Although she kept a healthy amount of teasing in her voice, inside Ivy felt sick to her stomach. Remembering that night with Eli just made her broken heart ache all the more. Her shoulders slumped, her fatigue suddenly became unbearable and her body fought to remain upright. "Look, Nelson. I'm afraid I'm not going to be very good company tonight. Sorry. I've got a lot on my mind and I'm super tired. I'm just gonna head home." She gave a small smile and turned to leave.

"Hey, hey, hey! Don't go running off!" Nelson put his arm around her shoulders. "I'm sorry about the dinner thing. It won't happen again." He raised one hand in the air. "Scout's promise."

Ivy couldn't help the light chuckle that escaped. "Were you even a scout?"

Nelson stepped back and put a hand to his chest. "Are you kidding me? Where the heck do you think I got all those amazing wilderness skills I use every day?"

Ivy folded her arms and smirked. "I thought scouts were trustworthy?"

"I am!"

Ivy raised an eyebrow.

Nelson put his hands on his hips. "We've had this argument before and you lost then just like you'll lose now. I've never lied to you."

Ivy grinned and shook her head. "Only because of your own interpretation."

"Semantics." Nelson waved her off. "There really are a group of us going to dinner, though. You should come."

"Is Eli part of this group?" Ivy held her breath.

"Nope. Just me and a few of the guys," Nelson said easily.

Ivy thought about sitting around with a bunch of loud, obnoxious men as they argued about everything from football to girls. *Yeah, that sounds like an enjoyable evening.* "Sorry, Nelson. I really am tired. Can I join you another time?"

Nelson sobered. "I really am sorry how everything has turned out, Fairy Girl. I feel responsible."

"Oh, no!" Ivy reassured him. "It's totally not your fault. Eli makes his own choices," she bit her lip to keep it from quivering, "and it just wasn't meant to be. I get it. It's okay."

"Ah, you're killin' me, Smalls!" Nelson stepped forward and wrapped his arms around Ivy, tucking her under his chin.

Ivy sniffled and laughed lightly. "I'm sorry. I don't mean to be such a baby. It's not like we ever really dated or anything, I shouldn't be so upset."

"Don't you apologize," he stated fiercely. "You're not to blame here, my bone-headed brother is. So, don't you dare be nice and say otherwise."

Ivy laughed again. "Thanks, Nelson."

Nelson pushed her back but kept his hands on her shoulders. "Tell you what, why don't you go grab your swimsuit and come relax in my hot tub while I'm gone tonight. It's the perfect night for it."

Ivy's eyes widened. "I couldn't do that! I've never even been to your house and that would be totally weird."

"Nah, nobody's going to be there. You can just sneak around back and soak your tired feet. I've even got a little fridge there with snacks and drinks and stuff."

Ivy narrowed her eyes at Nelson. "Why do I have the feeling you're trying to set me up again?"

Nelson rolled his eyes. "Fairy Girl, you are entirely too suspicious. But go ahead, ask me anything. You know I've never lied to you."

"Will Eli be there?"

"At my hot tub? No. Why would he be at my hot tub? He's got his own."

"Will he be at your house and somehow find me in the hot tub?"

Nelson grinned. "No. He will not be at my house."

"Can I bring someone with me? Like my roommate?" Ivy persisted.

Nelson put his hands out to either side. "Hey, bring whoever you want. Have a whole party if it would make you feel better. I'm just trying to do something nice for a friend."

Ivy's mind whirled. She couldn't think of anything else to ask him. He had point blank told her that Eli wouldn't be there and that was really her biggest concern. She softened her stance and smiled. "Thanks, Nellie. A nice soak does sound good. I just might take you up on the offer."

Nelson gave her a soft slug on the arm. "Sweet! You ever been to our cabins on the far side of the property?"

Ivy shook her head.

"'Kay. Just take that road," he pointed to a small graveled road that headed into the trees, "and keep going. There are only three turn-offs.

Mine is the first one. You can just park in the driveway. If you walk around to the left, then you'll run smack dab into the hot tub house. It's all glass, and the code is two-two-two."

"Well, that's easy enough," Ivy smiled. "Thank you for the offer. It's really sweet."

Nelson shrugged. "Eh. What are friends for? Oh, and you'll know you reached the right house if you see my red door."

Ivy felt a momentary jolt of panic. "Will Eli be able to see me at your house?"

"Nah. The houses are twenty acres apart. Not to mention all the forest between them." He shrugged. "I love my brothers, but geez, I want privacy too, sometimes."

Ivy smiled. "Great. Thanks. Have a good time tonight!" She waved and headed out the door to her car. A cool, crisp breeze nipped at her cheeks as she walked. *I have to admit it would feel amazing to soak in that hot tub tonight. Maybe I'll see if Heidi wants to go with me.*

CHAPTER 12

I vy drove slowly over the loose gravel road. It was hard to see in the dark and she bit her lip as she worked her way through the unknown area. A turnoff came up on her left and she drove into the driveway. Her lights flashed across the front of the house and she let out a sigh of relief when she spotted the red front door Nelson had spoken of.

"Made it," she muttered. She parked off to the side of the garage doors just in case Nelson got home early and turned off her car. Grabbing her bag and towel, she stepped out of the car and studied the home.

Ivy whistled low under her breath. "Geez, Nelson. Why do you ever bother to leave home?" The large, log beam mansion stood tall and intimidating in the darkness of the evening. Bright outdoor lights lit up the outside, but the blackened windows proved Nelson was gone as he had said.

Not for the first time, Ivy wished Heidi had come with her, but her roommate and friend had a date. *Which is way more important than hot tubbing it with a girlfriend who's feeling down.*

Cautiously, Ivy stepped around the side of the house, trying to not trip on anything. "There it is," she murmured as she rounded the back corner.

A large, glass gazebo stood in stark contrast to the wooden home. The light was on inside and the windows were steamed up. "Perfect," Ivy said as she shivered from the cool, evening wind.

Punching in the code Nelson gave her, Ivy made her way inside. The top was already folded off to the side, and the jets were bubbling in anticipation. "Thank you, Nelson." Ivy grinned and set her stuff on a nearby chair. Bending over, she gathered her hair into a large, messy bun on top of her head and walked toward the stairs.

"Ooooh, nice," Ivy moaned as she slid into the hot water. "I could get used to this." Closing her eyes, she lay her head back and let out a long breath. *This is just what I needed.*

ELI STOOD FROZEN AT the window as he watched Ivy punch in the code and walk into his hot tub room. *How-?*

A buzz in his back pocket made him jump, and he ducked away from the window as if Ivy would hear the sound. Grabbing the phone, he clicked on the message icon.

You can thank me later.

Eli's eyes strayed back out to the gazebo. He ran his hand through his hair. "How in the world did he get her to agree to come here?" His phone buzzed again, drawing his attention.

Don't screw this up.

Eli laughed harshly. "I'll try not to, Buddy. I'll try not to." Eli glanced down at his clothes. He had prepared the hot tub earlier for his own use, but hadn't gotten around to changing yet. *Do I go change or just talk to her like this?* He suddenly felt like a young boy with his first crush. "Get a grip man, you just need to apologize." Yet another buzz drew his attention.

Don't do anything I wouldn't do. Nelson sent a kissy-face emoji.

Eli rolled his eyes.

Shut up and leave me alone. Eli shot back.

Nelson sent a thumbs up.

Stuffing his phone in his back pocket, Eli straightened his shoulders and walked out onto the back patio. He could hear soft music coming from the gazebo and he chuckled. *Glad she's making herself at home.*

At the door, he stopped and wiped his sweaty hands on his jeans. His heart felt like it might pound out of his chest and Eli almost ran back to the house. *No. She's worth it.*

He took a deep breath, held it and opened the door.

Ivy was up to her neck in the water, resting with her eyes closed against the side of the tub. When she didn't stir at his entrance, he cleared his throat.

"Oh!" Ivy jerked upright. "AHHH!" She screamed when she saw Eli.

Eli's eyes widened, and he stumbled back at her reaction.

"Oh, no. No, no, no." Ivy closed her eyes and pressed her fists into them. "He said he wouldn't be here. Flat out said he wouldn't be here. No, no, no." Ivy leaped up, standing up in the water, glanced at Eli, down at her suit and then squealed and ducked back down in the water.

Eli stood frozen, unsure how to handle Ivy's fit. "Uh..."

Ivy shifted to the far side of the hot tub. "What are you doing here? Nelson told me you wouldn't be here. Why are you here?" Her voice was high pitched, and she spoke rapidly.

"I-" Eli tugged at his collar. "I wanted to speak with you. And why wouldn't I be here? This is my house."

Ivy stilled. "This is *your* house?"

Eli frowned and folded his arms. "Yes. Whose house did you think it was?"

"Nelson said-" she paused, closed her eyes and hung her head. "Nelson." Ivy shook her head. "I'm never speaking to him again."

Pain pierced Eli's heart. *It's too late. She hates me.*

Ivy schooled her features and straightened her shoulders. "Did you tell Nelson to tell me this was his house?"

"What?" Eli scowled. "No. I saw you come around into the hot tub and thought I would come talk to you."

Ivy narrowed her eyes. "You didn't wonder why I was wandering around your house at night?"

Eli shrugged. "Nelson sent me a text a few minutes ago. I figured it out."

Ivy groaned and threw her head back. "That meddling jerk has finally gone too far. He's a dead man."

Eli shifted his weight from foot to foot and ran his hand through his hair. Ivy's obvious anger had him rethinking his apology.

"So," she cleared her throat. "What did you want to talk to me about?"

Eli eyed her hugging herself in the water. Beads of sweat were starting to drip around her hairline, causing her curls to tighten and poke out around her exquisite face. "Do you want to..." He waved a hand toward the conversation area.

Ivy started to stand up, glanced down and promptly sat back down again. "No, thank you. I'll just listen from here."

"Okay." Eli cleared his throat. "I, uh... well, I-" He sighed and tugged on his collar again. "I wanted to say I was sorry," he finally blurted out. He glanced up at Ivy from under his eyelashes. Her face was a fixed mask. *I wish I could see what she is thinking.*

"I think you've already apologized, Eli," she said curtly. "I heard your explanation the first time."

"No," Eli shook his head. "I'm not sorry for that."

Ivy's jaw dropped.

"I mean, I am!" Eli threw his hands out, panic hitting him in the gut. "I am sorry about what happened a few weeks ago, but I'm sorry about more than that." He gripped his hair and stormed around in a circle. "Geez, I'm saying this all wrong." He spun and faced Ivy again. "I can't keep doing this, Ivy. I can't stand seeing you at work. I can't keep my distance. It's killing me."

"So... what?" Ivy's bottom lip trembled, and she sniffled. "Are you firing me? Telling me I need to work somewhere else?"

A brick fell in Eli's stomach. "No!" He sighed and walked over to the hot tub, leaning over the side. "I'm telling you I want to date you."

Ivy gasped. "You what?"

Eli reached into the water and grabbed one of her hands, pulling it out and kissing her knuckles. Her skin smelled of chlorine and felt hot against his lips and yet her touch still sent a shot of warmth to his core. "I want you to forgive me for being such an idiot and then I want us to explore this thing between us. I can't keep away, Ivy. I don't want to keep away."

Ivy's eyes had filled with tears and she was biting her lip. "Do you really mean that?"

Eli nodded, feeling some of his tension release now that she wasn't yelling at him. "Can you forgive me? I was wrong. I don't want to let my past dictate my future any more. I've never been as happy as I am with you. Please say you'll go out with me. That you'll give us a chance." Slowly, he pulled on her hand, dragging her over until she was kneeling right in front of him, with only the hot tub wall separating them.

He put his hands on her cheeks and leaned in close. "Please, Ivy. I'm so sorry for pushing you away. You'd think by my age I'd be smarter than this, but I can't seem to think straight when you're around."

Ivy hiccuped a laugh. "So you're saying this is my fault?"

Eli chuckled with her, leaning in until they were nose to nose. "No. It's definitely mine."

Ivy's misty eyes were filled with hope as she studied him. "I always was a sucker for a guy who could admit he was wrong." She chewed on her lip again.

Eli closed his eyes and rested his forehead against hers. "Is that a yes?"

"Yes," she whispered.

Eli's self control was gone. Being this close to her had his pulse racing and every time she bit that bottom lip he thought his knees were going to give out. "Thank you, Nelson," he muttered right before he took her mouth with his.

With her still in the hot tub, he couldn't get as close to her as he wanted. Letting his hands drop from her face, he slid them down to her waist and attempted to lift her out of the water.

Ivy squealed and jumped out of his hold, scrambling to the other side of the jacuzzi.

Eli ducked his head back and put up his hands to protect himself from the splashing water, but his clothes became soaked, anyway. "What did I do?" He asked, shocked at her response.

"I-I'm in my bathing suit! You can't just lift me out of the water!" Ivy was panting and put her hand over her chest as if she could slow the pounding of her heart.

Eli scrunched his face. "I'm lost."

Ivy sighed and leaned her head back. "Sorry. I just... I'm not ready for you to see me in my swimsuit yet."

"Why?" *Melinda took every opportunity to strut and show off every asset she had. What's the big deal?* "It looks like you're wearing a nice, modest one-piece. It's not like I'm going to see anything I shouldn't."

"Why?" Ivy jerked her head up, an incredulous expression on her face. "Why? I'll tell you why!" She glared at him.

Eli's eyes widened, and he stepped back. *Oh man, I'm so lost.*

"Because not all of us have perfect bodies with legs that go on for days or curves like Wonder Woman! Some of us are tiny and petite and that description can be used to describe everything about us, except maybe, when we've been eating too much ice cream because of stupid boys! Not to mention I'm in a granny suit that is more comfortable than flattering and now that you're finally admitting you were wrong, I don't want you to see me and change your mind!" Ivy huffed and splashed water at him.

You've got to be kidding me. She thinks I won't be attracted to her if I see her in an old bathing suit? Eli began to chuckle and when Ivy glared harder at him, he couldn't help himself. He leaned onto his knees and laughed harder. When he could catch his breath again, he stood and sighed. "Ivy Thompson. You are the most interesting girl I've ever met." He grinned and shook his head.

Ivy scowled and crossed her arms. "I fail to see what's so funny about this."

Eli walked around the hot tub until he was right next to her. Putting his hip on the built-in bench, he rested one arm on the side of the tub. Using his free hand, he tucked a wet curl behind her ear, then let his fingers linger on her neck. "For the record, I'm pretty sure your temper does not fall under that description."

Ivy scrunched her nose. "I don't actually get mad very often."

"Ah, so I'm just lucky." He tapped her nose. "Now, I thought we already went over how attractive I think you are."

Ivy's scowl remained. "I thought you wanted me to forgive you."

Eli jerked back a little. "I do."

"Then I think anything you said that night at the restaurant needs to be forgotten."

"Got it." He grinned at her. "Sweetheart, you are absolutely beautiful. I've thought so since the day you interviewed in my office. And as much as I love your kindness and personality, staying away from you wouldn't have been nearly so hard if you weren't so darn enticing. Keeping my hands to myself has become a major endeavor these last couple of weeks."

Ivy sighed and leaned into his touch. "I'm sorry I freaked out. It's just so hard to imagine this is real. You're gorgeous and rich and successful and I'm small and uneducated and a total charity case. How in the world can we make this work?"

"First off, you're not uneducated. You have an education, and if you wish to further it, you will get there someday. Slow progress is still progress. Second, you're not a charity case." He glared to make his point. "You have a job which you are very good at, with the world's best boss. What more could you ask for?"

Ivy laughed, and the sound vibrated through Eli's chest. "That might be a bit of a stretch."

"Come on," Eli stood. "Come out and let me hold you a while before it gets too late."

Ivy hesitated.

Eli put out his hand. "Do you trust me?"

After gnawing on her lip for a moment, Ivy's gaze met his. "I want to."

"Give me a chance to prove myself, Ivy. I know I was dumb and I'm sorry for that. But I've never felt this draw, this connection, we have. I know you feel it too." He held his breath as she sat debating his invitation. When she started to move toward the stairs, he let out a whoosh of air.

"Won't I get you all wet?" Ivy asked as she began to climb out of the tub.

"Trust me, a little water isn't enough to stop me from enjoying having you in my arms."

Eli walked over and grabbed one of his extra large, fluffy towels he kept in a cupboard. When he glanced back, Ivy was standing outside the tub looking nervous. Her arms were wrapped around herself and she kept shifting her weight from side to side. He glanced at her swimsuit and realized she was right, it was definitely not a show-off suit. The color was faded and the fabric obviously worn. It also appeared to be a size too big for her small frame. *Doesn't matter. It's her that's beautiful, not the clothes.*

Walking over, he wrapped the towel around her shoulders and used the edges to pull her into his body. He kissed her forehead and wrapped his arms around her. "Want to go in and watch a movie?"

Ivy looked up, her large, green eyes glistening. "I'd love to, but I don't have extra clothes."

Eli jerked his head toward the wall. "I've got robes you can wear. They'll also keep you warm."

"You just keep robes on hand for everybody?" Her jaw dropped.

Eli leaned in and nibbled at her ear. "Once in a while there are perks to being a billionaire."

Ivy laughed lightly and sighed. "I can see that."

Grabbing one of the robes. Eli wrapped Ivy up and led her inside.

IVY SIGHED IN CONTENTMENT and snuggled further in Eli's arms. They were currently sitting in his theatre room watching a superhero movie, but she had no idea what was going on. She was too focused on enjoying the way Eli kept rubbing her back or pushing his fingers through her hair. Every few minutes, he would lean down and kiss her head, almost as if he were just making sure she was still there.

"Are you warm enough?" Eli whispered in her ear.

"Mmm..." Ivy hummed. "Almost too warm. I'm so cozy I'm going to fall asleep if I'm not careful."

"We can't have that," Eli said as he nuzzled the side of her neck. "What do you think we should do to wake you up?"

Ivy giggled. "I'm open to suggestions."

The chuckle that rumbled through Eli's chest vibrated against Ivy's back and sent warm tingles running down her limbs. *Good grief, he's killing me. If I'm not careful, I'm going to be completely gone in no time.*

Eli pushed her upright, swung his legs over the front of the couch and pulled Ivy up into his lap. "Well, then it's a good thing I have some ideas," he whispered right before closing the gap between them.

Explosions and yells shot from the surround sound speakers placed strategically throughout the room they sat in, but Ivy was oblivious to it all. Wrapping her arms around Eli's neck, she pulled herself as close as she could get.

The large robe she wore put a thick barrier between the two of them and Ivy found herself frustrated she couldn't feel more of him.

Aaaand that's my cue to leave. Pulling back, she took a minute to catch her breath. "I should go home," she said breathlessly.

"I know, but a part of me is afraid you'll change your mind if I let you go."

Ivy grinned. Happiness soared through her at his change of heart where the two of them were concerned. "I think I'm the one who should be the most concerned about that."

"Touche," Eli murmured before kissing her hairline. "Will you spend tomorrow with me? You're not working, are you?"

"No, I have tomorrow off."

"Great. It's a date."

Ivy smiled. "I don't think I gave you an answer yet," she teased while running her fingers through his hair.

Eli closed his eyes, obviously enjoying her touch. "I don't think I should give you the chance to turn me down."

Ivy laughed softly. "All right, Mr. Boss Man. What did you have in mind?"

CHAPTER 13

I vy frowned as Eli brought the horse to her. "I don't think I trust Poppycock any more. Last time, he threw me off and ran away."

Eli chuckled and kissed Ivy's cheek. "I won't shout at you this time, so there will be no reason for him to do that again. I promise."

Ivy rolled her eyes. "Fine." Stomping over to the horse, she took Poppycock's face in her hands. "Alright, Buddy. Listen up. No funny business, all right? Last time it hurt to sit down for a full week, not to mention all the headaches. We're a team, got it?"

The horse blew out a huff of air and nodded his head up and down as if he understood every word.

"Great. Glad we had that little chat." Ivy smiled, walked to the side and patted her horse on her neck. Cocking her hip, she looked at Eli. "Ready?"

"As I'll ever be," he responded. "Although, I'm a little concerned with your ability to speak to horses. That wasn't on your resume." He hefted himself into the saddle and got comfortable.

Ivy shrugged before doing the same. "Yeah, well, horse whisperer wasn't exactly necessary for this job, plus I felt like it didn't leave me enough room to showcase my other fine qualities."

"Good to know," Eli nodded sagely.

Ivy smiled and laughed. "Okay, Cowboy. Let's go." Tapping her heels on Poppycock's side, Ivy started across the property toward the trail head.

Eli grinned and hurried after her. *I don't think I've smiled this much in years. Not even when I was still married. What is it about this tiny woman that makes me feel so... good?*

"Well, in another few months, your resort will reach its first year anniversary," Ivy smiled at him. "Congratulations, by the way." She winked.

Eli puffed up in his saddle dramatically. "Why, thank you," he spoke in a British accent. "We've worked hard to create something worth keeping around."

Ivy laughed. "You three did a good job." She glanced sideways at him. "I heard rumors you might be expanding. That seems really quick. Are they true?"

Eli scrunched up his face. "The gossip vine at the resort never ceases to astound me. How the heck do people hear about these things? I've only sat in on like two meetings!"

Ivy's eyes widened. "So it's true? Are you trying to build another resort somewhere else? Or restore another crumbling castle?"

Eli shook his head. "Nah. That was way too much work the first time." He looked at Ivy. "Do you remember that I once mentioned I have twin sisters?"

Ivy nodded.

"Well, since our parents are gone, my brothers, and I have been trying to convince our sisters to come out here to the resort with us. They both graduated recently and need jobs." He sighed and scratched the back of his neck. "Teagan has a degree in horticulture, so we told her she could oversee the grounds, but she loves growing and experimenting as well, so we've been talking about building her a greenhouse to do that, if she was willing to come out here to stay."

"Holy cow, that's generous," Ivy's jaw dropped.

Eli shrugged. "It actually makes good business sense, as well. We can grow fresh garden vegetables for Hayden's restaurant all year round, which will make him happy as well as my sister. This Washington weather doesn't have a very long growing season. So, it's a win-win."

"And what about your other sister? What's her name?"

"Laken. She's been a little tougher to convince. She and Teagan might be twins, but they are complete opposites." He grinned at his companion. "Teagan likes to work in the dirt all day, but Laken keeps her manicures sparkly clean. She went to cosmetology school, so it took us a while to figure out how to find something for her to do."

"And?" Ivy raised her eyebrows.

"We're talking of building a spa on the property and letting Laken run it."

"No way! A spa! Really? That's even better than the greenhouse!" She bounced in the saddle a little. "Will employees get a discount?"

Eli laughed and shook his head. "I take it you like facials and massages, huh?"

Ivy tilted head from side to side. "I've never actually *had* one, but I like the idea of them! What girl doesn't?"

"Teagan," Eli said with a grin. "Although," he frowned, "I think she stays away from that stuff mostly because Laken is so into it. Teagan is pretty quiet and prefers to stay in the background. Where Laken is more social and truth be told, she's kinda spoiled."

"Eh, having three older brothers will probably do that to just about any girl."

"True enough," Eli said with a nod. "Hey," pointed with his head to the side. "That meadow looks perfect. Lunch sound good?"

"Absolutely," Ivy said as she turned her horse toward the field of bright colored wildflowers and lightly, swaying grass.

AFTER GETTING OFF HIS horse, Eli walked around and helped Ivy. He put his hands around her waist and swung her out of the saddle as if she weighed nothing at all.

"Whoa!" She laughed and put her hands on his shoulders. "How is it," she squeezed his biceps, "that a guy who sits behind a desk all day has arms like this?"

Eli smirked. "Believe it or not, there's this place called a gym. Inside there are weights. If you-"

"Got it, got it." Ivy waved him off. "I just didn't realize you worked out all the time."

"I wouldn't say all the time, but I spend my fair share of time there." Eli reached into his saddle bag and grabbed a blanket. "Exercise has always been the factor that kept me sane. It's more about stress relief, than building muscles."

"Hm," Ivy nodded. "Have you always had a really stressful life? Like, before you became... famous?"

Eli shrugged and handed the blanket to Ivy, then reached back in the saddle bag to get their food. "About the same as anyone, I suppose. After the first couple of months, my marriage was more stress than enjoyment, so that gave me a reason to go. My job ended up being a dead-end, so that was another factor." Eli paused and glanced at her. "I guess I have always been a little on the high strung side."

Ivy grabbed his hand and started walking toward a flat expanse of grass. "Not today, you're not. Today, we're shoving everything else aside and just enjoying the fact that the sun is shining, and the wind is barely a breeze."

"Maybe so, but it's still only fifty degrees out," Eli pointed out.

"But the sun makes it feel warmer than that." Ivy spread out the blanket and Eli set down the bags of plastic containers.

Tucking her legs in and sitting on her hip, Ivy began to rifle through the bags. "So, what's good in here?"

"I think Hayden packed a couple of sandwiches, some pasta salad and chopped fruit. I told him to keep it simple."

"Awesome. Hayden makes fantastic food, simple or not." Once Ivy found the sandwich she wanted, she pulled it out and unwrapped it. "Oh yeah, super simple." She smelled the food before grinning at Eli. "This is Hayden's roasted chicken on his homemade ciabatta bread, and if I'm not mistaken, I smell a mustard aioli. Not to mention all the other toppings on here."

Eli's eyebrows shot up. "Wow. I'm impressed you figured all that out. Do you eat at the restaurant a lot?"

"Um... no." Ivy bit her lip and looked down. *Shoot. I don't want to tell him I can't afford to. I made that mistake last time.* "I just," she shrugged, "I might or might not have a small obsession with cooking shows. Plus, I hear people talk about the food at the front desk all the time."

"Wow. Hayden is a fantastic chef, we should go sometime." Eli grinned and took a bite of his own sandwich. "And I think you're right," he said after he swallowed.

Ivy held back her squeal at his use of the word 'we' and did her best to keep her cool. Instead, she reached over and patted his knee. "Might as well get used to saying those words."

Eli threw back his head and laughed.

Ivy smiled as she continued to eat. *That laugh has been waiting to be free for too long.*

"So," Eli began after a few moments of silence, "tell me about your family."

Ivy stiffened. "What exactly do you want to know?"

"Anything. Everything." He grabbed a container of salad.

Ivy took a big bite to stall while her mind worked furiously. *Well, my mother had cancer during my last year of high school and I barely graduated because I had to work and take care of her while trying to get my classes done. She then hung on for another three years before she died, while I set aside college and worked, leaving me in a mountain of medical bills that I am paying off as quickly as possible, but am not even close to being able to see light at the end of the tunnel.* "There's not much to tell," she lied. "I told you my dad's been gone since I was little and my mother died not long after I graduated from high school. I have no siblings and don't know of any extended family."

"I didn't realize it was quite that bad," Eli murmured sympathetically. "Was your mother the reason you didn't go to college right away?"

"Yep." Ivy dropped her eyes and began to pick at the fruit in her cup.

Eli reached out and put his warm hand on her forearm. "I'm sorry, Ives. I've always had a large, loud, overly affectionate family so I can't imagine what it must have been like to be on your own." He gave a little squeeze. "But it's obvious it didn't hold you back. You're pretty amazing."

Ivy felt her cheeks heat up, and she ducked her head. "Thank you," she murmured quietly. The happy feeling of a few moments before had disappeared and a heavy weight seemed to sit in the air.

"So..." Eli cleared his throat. "How 'bout them Mariners?"

Ivy scrunched her nose. "What?"

"That was a line we used to use during high school biology all the time." Eli grinned, then tilted his head. "Only it was the Angels. But my teacher was a huge baseball fan and if you piped up with that question, he'd almost always go off on some kind of tangent about how well or how terrible they were doing." Eli laughed. "We got out of more assignments that way."

Ivy giggled. "Nice. How many times were you the one to call out the question?"

"I plead the fifth," Eli grinned as he took another bite.

"So, you weren't always the quiet, grumpy guy in the corner, huh? It seems to me that Nellie would have been the troublemaker."

"Nellie," Eli chuckled. "I completely forgot you call him that. But anyway, Nelson was definitely the main trouble maker. The kid got sent to detention more times than I can count. But at one point in time, I was, believe it or not, a teenage boy and I think pretty much all of us are troublemakers in some way or another."

"I'll take your word for it." Ivy chewed a strawberry. "I didn't have any brothers. So I don't have much in the way of experience."

"Didn't you go on dates in high school? Or play a sport or anything? That would probably have given you more than enough experience to determine the lot of us are weirdos."

Dates and after-school activities become impossible when you have to work and take care of your mother. "Uh... nope. Never really dated." Ivy shrugged. "Ya know, I was the short, scrawny ginger. Not very appealing at that age. And although I enjoy the outdoors, I'm not a sports enthusiast."

Eli frowned and studied her for a moment. "I'm sorry. The more I hear about your growing-up years, the more I think you weren't very happy."

"Oh, no," Ivy hurried to say, "it was fine! My teenage years might have been a little... unconventional, but I wasn't unhappy. I'm sure I didn't miss out on anything that would have made a massive impact on my life. Besides," she took another bite of fruit, "I think the peek I got at my sporting skills in P.E. class were more than enough to say that I was not cut out for a team."

"What?" Eli put his hand to his chest. "Are you telling me that you wouldn't have been the star player on your school's basketball team? I find that hard to believe."

Ivy laughed at his dramatics. "What about you? What did you play?"

Eli's cheeks turned pink and Ivy's interest peaked. "Well, uh..." Eli rubbed the back of his neck. "I actually was a bit of a late bloomer. Didn't gain my height in time to work my way onto the basketball team or anything, so I joined the wrestling team."

Ivy's eyebrows shot up. "Wrestling? As in you wore those tight, spandex overalls?"

Eli groaned. "They aren't overalls! Why is it that those suits are always the first thing someone mentions when they think about wrestling? Nobody talks about the skill or strength involved. Nope. They only remember the uniform."

Ivy was smiling wide, now. "I can't," she giggled, "I just can't imagine you wearing something like that!" Her giggles turned into a full laugh and she held her stomach.

Eli huffed and rested his arms on his raised knees as he waited for her to calm down.

"Whew," Ivy wiped a tear from the corner of her eye. "That is definitely something I never would have guessed." Her head shot up. "Do you have any pictures?"

Eli glared. "No."

Ivy couldn't help the short laugh that bubbled from her lips at his pouting. "Oh, nevermind. I'll ask Nelson to find me- oh!" The breath whooshed out of her as Eli grabbed her and rolled them both to the side. His arms wrapped around her, cradling her head as he maneuvered the two of them until he had her pinned to the ground.

"You were saying?" He whispered against her ear.

Oh, heavens. I'm in way over my head. And I love it! She strained to lift her arms and fell back to the ground. "Dang, you're strong."

Eli gave her a deadpan expression. "It's not that hard to be stronger than you, Ivy. I'll bet I'm close to double your weight."

"Still..." She tried to buck him off, or move at all, but his hold was solid. "Good grief."

Eli chuckled as he watched her antics.

"Okay, okay. I won't ask Nellie for pictures. You win."

Eli leaned down until they were nose to nose. The air around them began to hum with anticipation and Ivy found her breathing becoming shallow. The pine needles and twigs that had been poking into her back only moments before were completely forgotten as Eli got closer.

"I think you owe me an apology," he murmured against her cheek. His lips began sliding along her skin, grazing her ear, then jaw line, leaving heat in their wake.

Every muscle in Ivy's body was frozen. "W-what?" She stammered.

"An apology, Ivy. You didn't even wait to hear that I was the state champion two years running, you went straight to laughing at me." He pulled his head back just far enough to look her in the eye. "Well, now you're paying the price. And I think a nice apology is in order."

"Apology. Right." Ivy's brain was struggling to overcome the fog that had settled in at his touch. "I'm uh, sorry. Yes. I'm sorry."

"Sorry for what?" He nipped at her earlobe.

"Hmm? I mean, yes. I mean, sorry. Yeah, sorry that I made fun of you." *Oh my word, I sound like a bimbo.*

Eli laughed against her neck before coming back up. "Are you sure that's what you mean?" His smile was wide.

"Mm, hm. Absolutely. That's what I mean." Ivy's eyes were locked on his lips. *Stop torturing me and just kiss me already!*

"Then, I accept." Finally, Eli let his lips drop to her own.

Each coiled muscle melted into a puddle of goo as Eli worked his magic on her. When he released her wrists, she wrapped them around his neck and let her fingers play with his hair.

After a few moments, Eli pulled back and scooted away from her. "You," he pointed at Ivy, "are dangerous to my self control."

Ivy sat up and crossed her legs. His words sent heat into her cheeks and she knew she looked like a ripe tomato. "Well," she grinned, "if I had known an apology was so intriguing to you, I would have tried that a long time ago."

Eli's laugh helped break up the heavy tang of desire still sitting in the air. He stood and brushed off his clothes before extending his hand. "Come on. It's probably time to get the horses back to the barn. Besides, it looks like another storm is rolling in."

Ivy took his hand and stood, then followed his lead in brushing off the dirt and debris. Glancing at the horizon, she noted the ominous black clouds closing in. "Oh geez, yeah. Looks like we better hurry, actually."

Together they put away their picnic and stuffed everything in the saddle bags.

"Up you go," Eli grunted as he put his hands around Ivy's waist and lifted her into the saddle.

"Whoa! I know how to do it, you know." She scowled at Eli to hide how much she enjoyed his show of strength.

"I know." He winked. "It was just a convenient excuse to touch you."

Ivy shook her head and smiled. "Well, come on Mr. Wrestler. Let's beat those clouds home."

Eli mounted and guided his horse up to her side. "After you, madam." He tipped an imaginary cowboy hat.

With a laugh, Ivy tapped her heels against Poppycock and pushed into a trot.

CHAPTER 14

E li waited until the customer Ivy was helping had walked away from the desk before he sauntered over. "Hello, Ms. Thompson," he said casually as he walked behind the front desk.

"Mr. Truman, nice to see you today," Ivy said with a bright smile.

Dang, I think she gets prettier every time I see her. Ever since he had apologized to Ivy in the hot tub a week prior, their whole relationship had changed. Eli felt lighter and happier than he had felt in years. He found himself finding reasons to come see her and couldn't seem to get enough.

Eli stepped up behind her as she typed at the computer. "Any troublesome customers today?" He whispered in her ear. Eli held back a grin as he watched a slight shiver run down her spine.

"Nope. All quiet on the western front, this morning." She glanced over her shoulder with a flirty grin. "Was there something you needed, Sir?"

"Now that you mention it, I find myself out of coffee. Do you happen to know how to fix that problem, Ms. Ivy?" Eli took in a deep breath, enjoying the smell of her hair and perfume.

"I think I can help with that. Should I bring it to your office?"

"That would be preferred, thank you." Nodding at the other front desk clerk, Eli tugged on his suit jacket and quickly marched back to his office.

IVY WATCHED HIM GO, biting her lip as she enjoyed the view of his tall, strong legs carrying him so quickly across the foyer.

"You better skeedaddle, girl," Janet teased. "He doesn't look like the patient type to me."

Ivy glanced over and her smile widened when the other woman winked at her.

"Hurry and get a good kiss for me while you're at it."

"Okay," Ivy nearly bounced over to the coffee center. *Thank you, Lord, for supportive coworkers.* Not every person at the resort had been as kind as Ivy's front desk companion.

Denton had made it clear he thought she was crazy and a few of the single, females who worked in other areas gave her nasty looks when no one was paying attention. But Ivy was too caught up in her new found happiness to pay them any mind.

She took a deep breath as she poured the hot brew. Her nervous excitement made her hands shake, and she feared she would spill boiling liquid everywhere. *That's just what I need. To ruin my clothes and the carpet before I go see the boss.*

Carefully, she carried the mug down the hall to Eli's open door.

Ivy peeked in, unable to see anyone. "Mr. Truman?" She asked as she stepped in. "Eli?" Ivy walked over and set the mug down on the desk then turned around.

Eli grinned from where he sat on the couch. "Hello, Beautiful."

Ivy felt her telltale blush blossom on her cheeks. "Hello, Handsome," she smiled back.

Eli stood and opened his arms while Ivy bounded into them.

"Mmm," Eli moaned. "I needed an Ivy fix."

She laughed lightly. "I thought you needed coffee."

"Simply a convenient excuse," Eli murmured into her hair. "You smell so good. Like sunshine and flowers. What the heck kind of shampoo is that?"

Ivy leaned back so she could look into his face. "Really? You called me in here to ask about my shampoo?"

"Absolutely not." Eli closed the distance between them, cutting off Ivy's laugh. After a moment, he buried a hand in her hair and deepened the kiss.

"Eli," Ivy breathed. *Good heavens, the man could kiss the socks off a kitten!*

"Hmm?" Eli kissed along her jawline, thrilled when Ivy tilted her head to offer him better reach.

"We better stop. I'm at work and my boss might discover me."

She felt Eli grin against her cheek. "Don't worry. I'll take care of him."

Ivy laughed lightly and put her hands on Eli's chest, creating a small distance between them. "I need to get back to work. Was there anything you needed besides a kiss?"

One side of Eli's mouth quirked into a grin and his grey eyes flashed. "Well, now that you ask-"

"Eli, behave," Ivy scolded, but her grin gave away her enjoyment of their flirting. With a reluctant sigh, she stepped back, breaking their connection "I was going to make fettuccine alfredo tonight," she bit her lip, "you, uh, you wouldn't want to come eat with me, would you?" *That was probably a dumb thing to ask. The guy is a billionaire! He's eaten at the finest restaurants in the world. Why the heck would he want to come eat pasta at my house?* Ivy's shoulders dropped along with her confidence and she opened her mouth to rescind the invitation when he spoke.

"I would love that." Eli's voice was husky and the sound of it caused Ivy to jerk her head up.

"Really?" She squeaked. "My roommate is going on a date, so I thought it might be nice to just... relax?" Her voice went up like a question rather than a comment and she held back a cringe at her nervousness. *Does every girl get nervous when they cook for their boyfriend the first time? Or is it only because he's rich and I'm afraid I'll disappoint him?*

Eli reached out and cupped Ivy's cheek. "I think a night in sounds wonderful. What can I bring?"

"Just yourself," Ivy said with a smile. "I'm not the world's best cook, but I promise not to poison you."

Eli chuckled. "I'll hold you to that promise."

"Seven, work for you? I have to work until six." Ivy grinned over her shoulder as she turned and headed toward the door. "My boss is a slave-driver."

Eli stuffed his hands in his pockets and rocked back on his heels. "Sounds like it. But seven is perfect. I'll look forward to it all afternoon."

Ivy bit the inside of her cheek to hold in a happy sigh. "Me, too," she whispered, then quickly slipped out the door before she did something stupid like run back into his arms.

Her coworker smirked when Ivy resettled herself behind the front desk. "Oh, knock it off," Ivy said with a laugh.

"I just hope you know what you're doing," Janet said. "I mean, you seem really happy, and that's great. I just don't want to see you get hurt, and he's kind of a big deal. He probably breaks hearts without even realizing it."

Ivy swallowed the retort that wanted to materialize on her tongue. *She's only looking out for me.* "I know," she reassured her friend. "I'm doing my best to go into this with my eyes wide open."

Janet nodded. "That's really all you can do." She patted Ivy's hand and went back to her job.

CHAPTER 15

Later that evening, Ivy felt like a chicken with her head cut off. She dashed around the apartment frantically trying to make things appear to their best advantage.

"The room is too dark, he's going to think I'm trying to like, seduce him or something," she muttered as she chewed her lip. Walking over, she grabbed the lamp and moved it to a different spot. "Okay, there. That will work... maybe... I hope. Ugh!" She threw her hands in the air. "It's exactly the same as it was before!" She grabbed her head between her hands. "I have got to get a handle on myself. Sheesh, go on a few dates and kiss a guy and suddenly he has me in knots."

The doorbell rang and Ivy gasped. Putting her hands to her stomach, she felt a sudden lurching and bent over. "Oh my word, I'm going to be sick." Gritting her teeth, she stood back up. "No. I'm a big girl. I've handled worse things than this. Feeding the man I'm dating is no big deal. If he walks away because I'm living in a dumpy, little apartment, then that's his loss."

Straightening her shoulders and her resolve, she walked over to the door and threw it open.

Eli's eyes widened at her fierce look. "Uh, hi." He had his hands in his pockets and he rocked back on his heels. Pulling one hand out, he looked at his watch. "Did I come at the wrong time or something? You look upset."

Ivy slumped and hung her head. "No. You're right on time. I'm sorry." She stepped back and waved her arm to let him in. After he had stepped through the door, she shut it behind him. "I've just been so worked up and nervous about having you come over." She scrunched up one side of her face. "I guess I had to put on my brave face to let you in and was a little too forceful."

Eli frowned and slowly reached out, gathering Ivy against his chest. She sighed at his warmth and snuggled in.

"Why were you so nervous? Have I done something to hurt you?"

"Of course not, but the few times we've been out we've gone to fancy restaurants, with fancy clothes and fancy food and now we're going to sit on my garage sale couch, and I'll be cooking for you with my non-fancy skills and serving you on non-fancy... stuff. I mean, I guess we went on that picnic and it wasn't fancy, but it was a picnic! They're not suppose-"

"Hey, hey, hey," Eli put his finger to her lips. "Did you think I would be offended by the fact that you aren't wealthy?"

"Maybe," Ivy admitted.

"Oh, Ivy," Eli chuckled and pulled her back in. "Don't you remember how I told you the story of the castle? How I was broke, and we threw everything we had into it? Well, before then, I worked my way through college. So, I know exactly what it's like to be a poor college student. Honestly, if I hadn't been able to donate plasma, I'm not sure if I would have had enough to eat some days."

"Really?" Ivy wrapped her arms around his waist and held on, enjoying how he made her feel so calm and safe.

"Really." He kissed the top of her head. "I wasn't born rich and I have no expectations that everyone else should be. In fact, when we were working on the castle, I had less than twenty bucks in my bank account. Total truth."

Ivy leaned back to look him in the eye. "Wow. That is cutting it close. So you really don't mind slumming it with me tonight?"

He chuckled again and gave her a quick peck on the lips. "I'm more comfortable on your garage sale couch than I think I will ever be on a fancy sofa."

Ivy smiled and stepped back, then took his hand. "Well then, come on Mr. Billionaire and enjoy the darker side of life."

"SOUNDS GOOD TO ME," Eli said as he followed Ivy the few steps to her kitchen. He glanced around as she stirred the pot on the stove. It was true that her apartment was anything but fancy, but it was neat and clean. *And homey. It feels lived in.* Satisfied and grateful for the chance to enjoy more time with her, Eli folded his arms and leaned against the counter.

"Is there anything I can do to help?" He asked as she scurried around the kitchen.

"Nope. All under control," Ivy said as she stuck her head in the fridge.

"You sure? Being a bachelor, I've learned my way around the kitchen, a little. I'm pretty darn good at following directions."

Ivy stood and put her hand on her hip, cocking her head. "Are you saying I get to boss you around tonight?"

Eli saluted. "Absolutely, Boss."

Ivy's melodic laugh vibrated through his chest and Eli had to hold himself back from closing his eyes to savor the sound. "What first?"

"Alrighty then, if you're going to help, why don't you grab the salad and get it all mixed together?" Ivy nodded toward the bag on the counter.

"Yes, Sir." He set himself up at the counter close to where she was working so that as she moved she had to work around him. Every time she put her hand on his back to reach something or leaned in close, it was absolutely the best torture he had ever been through.

"I think you did this on purpose," Ivy teased as she leaned over his shoulder yet again for a bottle of spice.

"I don't think I should dignify that with a response," Eli winked at her.

"Clever boy," Ivy murmured.

Eli frowned. "I stopped being a boy a long time ago."

Ivy let her eyes run over him from head to toe. Pursing her lips she nodded. "I can see that."

"You're lucky my hands are dirty, or I might just grab you and have my way with you," Eli said with a raised brow.

Ivy leaned in over his back and put her lips to his ear. "Maybe I'll let you."

When she tried to back away, Eli spun and grabbed her around the waist. "You're playing with fire, Little One."

"Who you calling little? I'm just as much of an adult as you are."

Eli let his eyes travel down her the same way she did him moments ago. "I think maybe you forgot to finish growing, though."

Ivy gasped in mock outrage and swatted his shoulder. "Maybe you just over grew. Ever think of that? Huh?"

Grinning, Eli leaned back against the counter and pulled her closer. "Or maybe I think you're just the perfect size." He gave in to the urge he had had since he arrived and gave her a sweet, soft kiss. He had planned to pull back, but that little taste of heaven wasn't nearly enough. Wrapping his arms all the way around her, he deepened the kiss. It lasted only moments before the oven timer dinged, and Ivy jerked in his arms.

Breathing heavy, she stepped back, her eyes focused on him. "I have to get the bread or it will burn."

Eli nodded but didn't speak.

Grabbing a hot pad, Ivy opened the oven door and pulled the foil-wrapped package out and onto the counter. The smell of butter, yeast and garlic filtered through the air and caused Eli's stomach to rumble in response.

Ivy grinned. "Well, good to know you're hungry."

Eli grinned back. "I might be hungry for more than just food."

The flush that crawled up Ivy's neck and into her cheeks only made her more attractive. Holding back a groan, Eli turned around and picked up the salad bowl. "You want this on the table?"

"Yes, please," Ivy said as she took the pot full of pasta to the sink to drain.

"That wasn't very boss-like," Eli said over his shoulder.

"I'm sorry. How about... right now! Chop, chop!"

"Better." Eli smirked. "We'll make a sergeant out of you yet."

Ivy laughed. "Let me toss this with the sauce and then we can eat, okay?"

"Perfect."

After they finished eating, Eli patted his stomach and leaned back in his seat. "That was delicious." He frowned at Ivy. "I thought you said you weren't very good in the kitchen."

Ivy shrugged. "It's not that I can't cook, but I'm pretty simple in what I do. Pasta, hamburgers, tacos, you know, the stuff that everybody can do."

"My mom always said that doing simple things well was better than doing big things poorly."

"She sounds like a wise woman," Ivy rested her chin on her hand and smiled at him.

Eli felt that warmth and contentment that only Ivy brought work its way through his chest again. *How does she do that? No one else has ever made me feel so, so... peaceful.*

Mimicking her position, he grinned at her. "Thank you, for dinner," he whispered.

"Anytime," Ivy murmured back. "Did you have plans for the rest of the evening?"

Eli grinned. "Are you trying to get rid of me?"

Ivy sat up straight. "No! Absolutely not! I-" She stopped when she realized Eli was chuckling. "You. You always do that!" She swatted at him and he caught her hand.

"And you always fall for it." He played with her fingers, enjoying their delicate softness. "Did you have something you wanted to do this evening?"

Ivy's cheeks turned pink again and Eli held his breath, wondering what she would say.

"Oh, I definitely have something I'd like to do with you, but we shouldn't do it."

Eli raised a single brow. "Really? And why is that?" He kissed her fingers.

Ivy sighed. "Because it could lead to trouble."

"Maybe trouble isn't so bad," Eli tugged on her hand, pulling her up from her seat, then down into his lap.

"Trouble is bad," Ivy explained as she ran her fingers through his hair. "That's why it's called trouble."

Eli closed his eyes, enjoying her touch. "So, what do you propose?"

Ivy pursed her lips for a moment. "How about a game?"

Eli's eyes popped open. "A game?" He frowned.

"Yep!" Ivy leaned in and touched her nose to his. "I happen to be the queen of Monopoly."

Eli's eyebrows went up. "The queen, huh? And how did you manage to obtain that title?"

Ivy shrugged coyly and stood up. "I may or may not be undefeated in this particular game." She grinned over her shoulder as she walked to the hall closet. After retrieving the long box, she walked over to the coffee table. "Come join me." She patted the seat on the sofa next to her.

Eli narrowed his eyes and watched her for a moment. Slowly, he stood up and came over the couch. He sat down and leaned over to her ear. "I had other plans for us tonight." He smirked when he saw a patch of goosebumps cover her skin.

Ivy cleared her throat. "Maybe so, but we can't just kiss all evening, Eli."

Falling back into the couch, he crossed his arms. "Why not?"

Ivy looked over at him and laughed. "You look like a child that lost his favorite toy."

"I did."

Ivy closed her eyes and shook her head. "I like kissing you as much as you enjoy kissing me-"

"Obviously, not," Eli grumbled.

Ivy pinched her lips and shot him a glare. "But the truth of the matter is, we don't know that much about each other yet. We need to spend time learning about each other, too."

"And playing Monopoly helps this how?" Eli raised a single eyebrow.

"Have you never played the game?" She turned sideways on the couch and tilted her head. "Trust me. You learn more about a person while playing Monopoly than in a whole slew of dates."

Eli gave her a skeptical look, then sighed. "Fine. You want to play a board game, we'll play a board game."

Ivy squealed and kissed his cheek while he continued to grumble good naturedly under his breath.

"Hey now, no starting something you already said we couldn't do."

Ivy gave a flirty little grin. "I didn't say we couldn't kiss. I just said it shouldn't be all we do. After the game is over, we can kiss and make up."

Eli paused, his hand hovering over the board. "Why would we need to make up?"

Ivy laughed. "You'll see."

Two hours later, Eli threw his hands in the air. "That's it! I'm bankrupt."

Ivy smiled wide and rubbed her hands together. "Awesome! Another win in the books! I'm still the queen!"

He folded his arms. "I don't know how you did it. One minute I thought I was doing great, the next I owed you two thousand dollars. What's your secret?"

"Uh, uh, uh." Ivy ticked a finger at him. "A queen never reveals her secrets."

Ivy gasped when Eli grabbed her around the waist and pulled her onto his lap. Wrapping one arm tightly around her, he held his other hand at her side. "Maybe I'll tickle it out of you," he whispered in her ear.

"I'm not ticklish," Ivy whispered back.

Eli jerked back. "What? Isn't everyone ticklish?"

She shrugged. "Not everyone apparently. I've never been."

"Well, shoot." He laid his arm across her legs. "There goes my bargaining chip."

Ivy leaned in nose to nose. "I'm sure a big, strong man like yourself can find other ways to get what he wants."

He gave her a small peck. "Oh yeah? I thought I wasn't allowed to do that?"

"I told you after the game we'd kiss and make up."

"Right." He gave her a little longer kiss. "Why do we need to make up?"

"Because you got beat by a little, itty, bitty girl." Ivy kissed his jaw.

Eli threaded his hand through her hair. "I'll let you beat me every night if this is what I get."

Ivy gasped. "You didn't let-"

Before she could get the rest of her argument out, Eli leaned in and put her lips to a much better use.

CHAPTER 16

Want to go on a ride on Sat? I want to show you the lake.
Ivy grinned as she read the text on her phone. Several days had gone by since she and Eli had had dinner at her apartment, and things had been so busy she had hardly seen him.

That sounds like fun. Think the monopoly board would fit in the saddle bag?

Better not chance it. It might conveniently get lost and then you'd never see it again.

Ivy laughed quietly. **Fine. I guess we'll just have to find something else to keep us busy.**

;) Sounds good to me. Meet me at the barn at eleven.

Done deal.

Ivy tucked her phone back in her pocket with a smile on her face. Never before had she felt so carefree. Being around Eli seemed to make her burdens more manageable. She had missed so much of her growing up in order to take care of her mother and even though she was gone, Ivy was still bearing the load left behind. *But Eli makes me feel like everything is going to be okay. Like I can do anything.*

"Things must be going okay," Janet said from the far side of the small area they worked in. "You've got that twitterpated look on your face." She grinned. "Ah, new love. I remember when I was acting the exact same way."

"Love?" Ivy's jaw dropped. "I don't love him, we've only been dating a few weeks!"

Janet frowned. "Oh hon, you've been floating on cloud nine for days now." She shrugged. "I'm not saying you're going to marry him, but you've definitely fallen for him. First love doesn't always turn out to be the right one."

Ivy chewed her lip. *Do I love him? And would that be a bad thing if I did? Are his feelings as strong as mine?*

As if she could hear Ivy's thoughts, Janet continued. "It's not like he doesn't feel the same way. We've all noticed how much he has softened since you two got together." Janet wrapped an arm around Ivy's shoulders and squeezed. "He actually smiles now and is much more friendly to the staff. He's fallen just as hard as you have."

The thought of Eli loving her sent a burst of excitement through Ivy. She could just imagine being able to spend time with him every day rather than scheduling bits and pieces here and there. *If we got married would he want kids?* She could picture a little boy running around their house with her red hair, but Eli's alluring grey eyes. The thought sent a bolt of yearning through her so strong, it stole her breath, only to be followed by a sinking despair when she thought about what she was still hiding from him. *I just don't want him to think I'm after his money. Or that I'm some charity case. Is that so bad?*

She pushed those thoughts away and turned to Janet. "We haven't even come close to saying we love each other."

Janet squeezed Ivy's shoulders one last time and then shrugged when she dropped her arm. "That's okay. It'll happen when it happens. You can't rush these things, Hon. Especially for the men. They usually take longer to realize the depth of their feelings than a woman. Give him time."

Ivy chewed her lip and nodded. *Time. Just give him time. I can do that. It'll all work out how it's supposed to.*

"HOW GOES IT, LOVER Boy?" Nelson sauntered into Eli's office at the end of the day on Friday and plopped himself onto one of the chairs. Dust puffed from his clothes and Nelson coughed while waving his hand through the air.

"What are you doing?" Eli glared at his dirt ridden brother. "Where the heck have you been that you are that dirty?"

"Camping," Nelson said with a shrug. "Just got back. Wind kicked up on us and everyone came home more covered in dirt than clothing." Nelson slapped his hand across his thighs, knocking dirt everywhere.

"Stop!" Eli stood. "Why don't you go home and take a shower or something?" He sighed and collapsed in his seat. "Now I'm going to have to ask the maids to come in and clean this up."

"Sorry." Nelson coughed again. "I just wanted to see how things were going between the two lovebirds. Then I'm heading to my home, where I shall sleep in my own bed, shower in warm water and not emerge until Monday."

"Quit calling us lovebirds, we've barely started our relationship. And you're the one who wanted to start up those outdoor excursions. Getting dirty and sleeping on the hard ground is your own fault." Eli tapped his pencil against his desk.

"I think Mother Nature is just out to get me. I swear there were twice as many rocks as usual at the campsite," Nelson grumbled, shifting his shoulders around.

Eli laughed. "Or, maybe you're just getting old, Little Brother."

"Old, schmold," Nelson grinned back. "If I'm getting old, that makes you ancient."

"True enough," Eli acknowledged the hit. "What exactly did you need again?"

"I was seeing how the love story was going," Nelson smirked.

Eli rolled his eyes. "Stop using that word."

"What? Love?"

"Yes. It's way too early for something like that." Eli tilted his chin down and raised his eyebrows.

"Says who?" Nelson folded his arms and more dirt fell on the chair.

Eli scrunched his nose, but Nelson ignored him.

"You know as well as the rest of us that you two are in love with each other."

"Knock it off," Eli waved the comment away with his hand.

"Okay, I'll prove it to you." Nelson sat up straight. "One," he put one finger in the air, "you smile all the time now. Two," a second finger popped up, "you can't stop watching her when you're in the same room. Three, you laugh about nothing at random times. Four, every time you're close to her you have to touch her. Five-"

"I get your point!" Eli shouted over Nelson explanation. "But none of those things mean I'm in love. Don't all men get that way at the beginning of a relationship?" The room suddenly felt warm and Eli tugged at his tie. *I can't be in love with her all ready? Can I? I'm not ready for that. Love leads to marriage. Marriage leads to divorce. There's no way I want to go through that again.*

Nelson leaned forward, leaning his elbows on his knees. "Were you that way with Melinda?" He asked quietly.

Eli froze. *No. I was content with Melinda, but I never felt this stupid-happy feeling I get with Ivy. Melinda never felt like home.* He clenched his jaw. No matter what thoughts were running through his brain, he was not going to admit them out loud to Nelson.

Nelson stood and stretched, knocking off yet more dirt. "You don't have to say it, we can all see it. And I'm happy for you. Don't screw up again though, hmm?"

"Whatever," Eli grumbled. "Get out and take your dirt with you."

"Too late!" Nelson laughed as he walked out the door. "What the heck are you doing here?" Nelson's angry shout came through Eli's open door.

Eli jerked toward the sound.

"I'm here to see my husband," a sultry, feminine voice answered.

Eli felt like he had been socked in the gut. *Melinda!*

"Ex-husband." Nelson answered. "Or do you not understand what a divorce is?"

Melinda laughed lightly.

Eli put a hand to his chest. Not too long ago the thought of hearing Melinda laugh again would have sounded appealing. There had been too little of that in their relationship, but the pain he expected never came. Instead, Eli found himself getting angry.

"What does she think she's doing, walking into our hotel?" Shoving thoughts of Ivy and love out of his mind, he stood and began to march across the floor.

The sounds of shouting were getting louder and Eli quickened his stride. "They're going to bring the whole resort running."

"Don't touch me!" Melinda jerked her arm away from Nelson.

"You can't go in there!" Nelson shouted over her.

"What do you think you're doing?" Eli growled when he got into the hall.

Both Nelson and Melinda froze and turned to stare at Eli. Nelson's face was a mask of hatred while Melinda quickly tempered her features into a practiced smile.

Feelings of betrayal and inadequacy slammed into Eli's chest and for a moment he couldn't breathe. When he could finally fill his lungs, he glared at the pair in front of him.

"Bring this into my office before you disturb the guests," Eli demanded.

Shooting Nelson a smug look, Melinda strutted the rest of the way down the hall, but not before giving Eli a coy glance as she walked past him. Disgust rolled through Eli and he barely held back from rolling his eyes at her antics.

Nelson hadn't moved and Eli raised a brow at him.

"I don't think I can go in there and be civil," Nelson admitted in a growl.

Eli nodded. "Fine. You need to go shower, anyway. I'll be fine."

Nelson stared at him for a minute. "Don't screw this up," he said curtly, then spun on his heel and took off.

Eli watched him go and once Nelson was out of sight, his eyes automatically drifted to the front desk. To his disappointment, no ginger-haired fairy met his gaze.

"Eli, are you coming?" Melinda's impatient question broke Eli's stare, and he turned toward the doorway.

Without saying a word, Eli walked in and closed the door, then proceeded to his desk. He sat down and took his time situating himself and organizing the papers on his desk.

Melinda folded her arms across her chest and began tapping her toes. "Are you quite finished?"

Putting on the icy facade he had become known for, Eli leaned back in his chair and raised a brow. "Ready for what? Why exactly are you here?"

"Aren't you going to ask me to sit?" Melinda tilted her head and smiled. "I remember you as having better manners than this, Eli."

"I don't anticipate you being here long enough for you to need to sit. And I repeat, what are you doing here?"

With a huff, Melinda stomped over to the chair and sat down. Dust puffed around her and she jumped up again. "What? What kind of shoddy resort are you running here? I would have thought you had enough money to make sure this place was spotless."

Eli couldn't help the small ping of satisfaction he found in seeing Melinda covered in dust. She was always so meticulous about how she looked and it appeared as if time hadn't changed that. Her nails were long and shiny and her hair sleek and long. Her clothes fit her like a glove, showing off every curve and meant to entice any man she came across. Her skirt ended at mid-thigh and the amount of tanned leg between the skirt and her high heels appeared to go on forever.

"I'm afraid you chose the chair that Nelson sat in right before you arrived. Now, did you come to complain about the resort or did you have something else in mind? Because I'm afraid I don't have time to sit and reminisce with you this evening."

After Melinda brushed the last of the dirt off of her, she carefully checked the other chair before sitting down. "That's better."

"I mean it, Melinda. Get to the point or get out." Eli was losing control of his anger and he wanted her gone.

"Hmm. You don't seem happy to see me, husband. I expected at least a 'hello'."

Eli grabbed his phone and punched in a single number. "Security? I need you in my office right away."

Melinda stood and sauntered to the desk. "Now, Eli. There's no need for that." She rested her hip on the edge of the desk and toyed with a glass paperweight sitting nearby. "Why are you so against talking to me? If I didn't know any better, I would think you're hiding the fact that you still love me with your anger."

Eli looked at her in shock. "You've got to be kidding me. Any feelings I foolishly had for you flew out the window years ago. Even before the divorce."

Melinda frowned. "Now, there's no need to get nasty."

The door opened behind her and two security guards walked in.

"Well, looks like my time is up for today."

The men started toward her but paused when Melinda put up her hand.

"Now, gentlemen, no need to get physical. I'm coming." She stood and glanced over her shoulder. "I'll see you in the morning," she said casually.

"You will not. We have nothing to talk about, not to mention I have an appointment tomorrow."

"Cancel it. We need to talk." Melinda spun and glared at him.

"I don't think so," Eli said cooly.

"What's the matter, got a hot date?" Melinda smirked. When Eli didn't answer, her jaw dropped, then she threw back her head and laughed. "Oh, that's rich. The non-dating billionaire has a date, just as his wife comes back into town."

"Stop it," Eli growled. Putting his hands on his desk, he stood. "Ex-wife. And don't forget it."

Melinda shrugged. "Tomato, tomahto. You need to cancel the date and might as well cancel the lucky, little lady all together. Don't want to get her hopes up." She turned and walked to the door.

"Why are you here, Melinda?" Eli's voice has risen to match his temper, and he clenched his fists in an effort not to strangle the woman in front of him.

Melinda paused, her hand on the door frame and looked back. "I'm here to get what I deserve, Eli. My share of the treasure." Before Eli could respond, Melinda winked and disappeared.

Eli's knees shook, and he collapsed in his chair. "She can't be serious," he mumbled. A flicker of panic began in his chest. Before it could become a roaring flame, he grabbed his phone and called Hayden.

"Kinda busy right now!" Hayden shouted over the noise of the kitchen. "It's the dinner rush, this better be an emergency."

"Melinda was here," Eli stated bluntly.

Hayden cursed. "What did she do?"

"She wants the money."

The noise of the kitchen continued coming over the phone, but Hayden was silent.

"Can you get away later?" Eli asked.

Hayden sighed loudly. "Yeah. Let me know when."

"Let me get a hold of Nelson and I'll shoot you a message."

"Fine." Hayden hung up.

Eli groaned and ran his fingers through his hair. Next, he dialed Nelson.

"Dude, is the witch gone?"

"Gone from my office. But not forever. She wants to talk to me tomorrow."

"About what?"

"She wants the money."

"You've got to be kidding!" Nelson growled. "She has no right to it."

"Yeah well, she obviously thinks she does, or she wouldn't be here." Eli slumped back in his seat, resting his head back and closing his eyes.

"What are we going to do about it?"

"Can you meet later tonight? I know you're tired, but this is important."

"Yeah. I've gone without sleep before."

"Thanks," Eli sighed. "Let's plan on nine, that way Hayden can find someone to cover."

"I'll be there."

"Sounds good."

Once they had hung up, Eli's finger hovered over the next person he needed to call. His finger shook and his mind spun in circles as he tried to figure out what to say to her. Dropping his phone, he put his face in his hands. *I can't tell her my ex is here. Our relationship is too new. What would she say if she knew I was blowing her off to talk to Melinda? But I can't lie to her either. I'm just going to have to man up and hope she forgives me.*

He shook his head, then groaned when it doubled his headache. With stiff movements, he picked up the phone and pressed her name.

"Hey, Handsome! I'm so excited for our date in the morning! I've totally been checking the weather forecast, and it looks like it's going to be perfect." Ivy's sweet, soprano voice felt like a soothing balm, but her words were a knife to Eli's heart.

He couldn't do it. Despite one side of his brain screaming that he was a chicken, Eli knew he couldn't tell her the truth. "Hey, Sweetheart. I'm afraid I've got bad news."

"What's the matter? Are you okay?" Ivy's tone had dropped and her concern was easily heard.

Blowing out a breath, Eli answered. "Not really. I've got a major migraine and I don't think I'll be able to make it in the morning. Can we do a rain check?" *At least that wasn't a complete lie.*

"Of course!" Ivy reassured him. "Your health is way more important than our date. I've never had a migraine before, but my mo- never mind. I've heard they're terrible. How can I help? Can I bring you dinner tonight?"

Shoot. "Uh, no, thanks. That's really nice of you, but I think I need to just go to bed. I've got a prescription that knocks me out and I'll plan on sleeping in in the morning and hopefully between the drugs and the rest, it will go away." Eli closed his eyes and pinched the bridge of his nose.

"Okay. I'm so sorry you aren't feeling well. I'll just plan on getting caught up on my homework tomorrow, instead."

"Sounds good. Thanks." Eli felt his stomach lurch. *I've got to get off this call or I'm going to end up telling her everything.*

"Sleep well. I'll talk to you soon."

"Yep. You too." Eli quickly disconnected the call before his conscience could get the better of him. "It's better this way," he mumbled. "We'll take care of this and she'll never have to know."

Stuffing everything he thought he might need in his briefcase, Eli stormed out of his office, dialing his lawyer along the way.

CHAPTER 17

"She said what?" Hayden shouted and jumped out of his seat. His knee bumped the table they were gathered around and his can of soda toppled over.

"Shoot." Eli jumped up and grabbed some paper towels. "Knock it off, Hay. Ruining my floors isn't going to help the situation."

"Sorry." Hayden paced around the table with his hands in his hair.

Eli eyed his brother as he mopped up the sticky mess. Hayden's voice had actually been contrite, which was an unusual emotion for the overbearing brother.

"What I don't get," Nelson said as he took a sip of his own drink, "is why she thinks she has any right to it. You two were already divorced when everything went down, so what does she think she can do to get her hands on the money?"

Eli shrugged and sunk back into his seat after tossing the towels in the garbage. "I have no idea. She just dropped that bomb and waltzed out. I have no doubt that she knew what it would do to me to hear those words."

"So, she's purposefully trying to make you panic," Hayden said as he slid back into his seat.

"Probably."

"Is there someone we can call to look into things for us?" Nelson asked

"I've already contacted our lawyer. He's going to go back over everything and make sure there's nothing we missed in the government paperwork and stuff. But until he does that, I got nothing."

Nelson yawned loudly.

"Okay, so we all stay on alert for the snake. She isn't allowed to hang around the property or anything. And tomorrow morning, Eli will meet with her and figure out what she's got up her sleeve. Right?"

"I thought you had a date with Ivy tomorrow?" Nelson folded his arms and rested his head back on the chair.

"I did. I canceled," Eli mumbled, keeping his eyes on his glass.

Nelson opened one eye and looked at him. "How did she feel about Melinda being here?"

Eli pinched his lips but didn't answer.

Nelson sprang forward. "You didn't tell her, did you?"

Eli shook his head.

"You realize that's going to come back to bite you in the butt, right? There's no way she's not going to find out what's going on. All it would take is one word from Melinda to the media and this whole story, true or not, is going to be on every major newspaper in the world."

Eli rubbed his hands down his face. "I know, okay? I had planned on telling her, but when it came down to it, I couldn't do it. I knew it would hurt her. She sounded so happy when we were talking that I just..." He blew out a breath. "I couldn't do it. I mean, how would you feel if the woman you were dating canceled your day together because her ex came into town." Eli shook his head. "No matter how innocent it is, it just looks and sounds wrong. I won't put her through that unless I have to."

Nelson shook his head, his jaw was clenched and his eyes hard. "Next time you have to grovel, I'm out of it. She deserves to hear the truth from you and if you can't man up and say something, then you don't deserve her."

"I don't want your help, you shouldn't have interfered to begin with," Eli growled.

"Whatever, Man." Nelson stood and headed toward the door. "Let me know how things go with Crazy Lady tomorrow." Walking out into the darkness, Nelson slammed the door behind him.

"He's right. You need to tell her." Hayden's voice was soft but firm.

"What do you know?" Eli lashed out, pushing himself away from the table. "I don't see you in any lasting relationships." Without waiting to see his brother out, Eli headed toward the stairs and his bedroom.

What I need is a handful of aspirin and a long night's sleep. Ivy is better off in the dark for now.

CHAPTER 18

Ivy couldn't concentrate on the homework in her lap. Her thoughts were consumed with Eli and how down he sounded on the phone last night. She glanced at the clock on her phone. "Ten." She blew out a breath through her lips. "Even if he was sleeping in, he should be awake by now." She chewed her lip. "Maybe I could drop him off some cookies and check on him. A little sugar always goes a long way."

Plan in place, Ivy jumped up and grabbed the cookie dough she and Heidi kept in the freezer for emergencies and quickly popped a batch in the oven. While it cooked she ran to the bathroom and freshened up.

Thirty minutes later, warm cookies in hand, she was on her way to Eli's cabin. Once at the resort, she drove around to the road that led to the brother's living areas on the backside of the acreage.

Pulling up in front of Eli's log mansion, she scrambled out, clutching the plate in her hands. Butterflies danced in her stomach at the thought of getting a little treat of her own.

Ivy practically bounded up the front porch steps, then rang the doorbell. She shifted her weight from one side to the other as she waited for Eli to answer. When a couple of minutes went by and no one came to the door, Ivy's excitement dropped.

"Is he still in bed?" Pulling her phone out of her pocket, she glanced at the time. "There's no way Eli is still lying around at this point." Making a fist, she knocked hard on the door.

Finally, Ivy heard the shuffling of footsteps. She frowned. *Those aren't Eli's steps.*

"Can I help you?" A tall, thin, older woman stood in the doorway.

"Uh," Ivy blinked a few times. "I was, um, looking for Eli. Is he still sleeping?"

"Oh, no. Mr. Truman has been up for hours. I'm Mrs. Whitworth, the housekeeper."

"Oh!" Ivy felt the tension begin to drain from her shoulders until she realized what else the woman had said. "He was up hours ago? Is he not home? I thought he had a migraine?"

Mrs. Whitworth frowned. "I don't know anything about a migraine, but he was gone by the time I arrived this morning. My instructions said he was at the office and would be home later." She glanced at the plate in Ivy's hands. "Would you like me to give him those?" She nodded toward the cookies.

"No, thanks. I think I'll head up to the office and deliver them in person. Thank you." Ivy smiled, but it felt strained. She spun on her heel and darted back to her car. The soft fluttering of the butterflies in her stomach from only moments before had turned into a swarm of stinging bees. *Something is not right, here.* Her gut churned, and she hurried down the road toward the castle.

Parking at the back of the lot so she didn't block any customers, Ivy once again grabbed her plate of cookies and walked into the building. She smiled and waved at some of her coworkers, doing her best to hide the tension radiating through her body. Her muscles coiled tighter and tighter the closer she got to Eli's office.

As she walked down the hallway, she noticed his door was ajar. As the noise from the foyer faded, she could hear voices coming from inside. Ivy stopped and chewed her lip. *Maybe I should just drop the cookies at the front desk and leave. He's probably in some type of emergency business meeting.*

Just as she started to turn around, she heard a throaty, yet distinctly feminine laugh come from the open door. Ivy froze. *He's with a woman?* Her heart dropped, but she quickly reprimanded herself. *Women work in the resort business too. Just because she's a woman doesn't mean it's not a business meeting.*

Her little pep talk did little to lift her spirits. Slowly, Ivy inched her way up to the door, leaning against the stone wall to stay out of sight. The feeling of doom that had followed her from the cabin became an almost unbearable weight.

Holding her breath, she leaned in as close as she dared.

"The documents show otherwise," the woman said.

"If you'll email them to me, I'll send them to my lawyer," Eli responded shortly.

Ivy let out a breath of relief. *See?* She chided herself. *It is a business meeting.*

"I thought maybe I could deliver them in a more personal way," the woman purred.

Ivy jerked upright and covered her mouth to hold in a gasp, nearly dropping her cookies in the process. Her ears strained to hear Eli's response, but only silence came from the room.

"Come now, we both know how you still feel about me. Why not just admit it?" The woman's voice had dropped into a sultry, melodic tone and Ivy couldn't take anymore.

Spinning on her heel, she practically sprinted back to her car. Once inside, she threw the plate on the passenger seat, not caring that the cookies spilled all over the fabric cover.

Cranking the engine, she tore out of the parking lot. Her mind spun at what she had heard and her vision clouded with tears. A sharp pain radiated through her chest and she put a hand on her heart, rubbing the spot.

"He lied to me. He outright lied to me." Ivy held back the sob that wanted to escape. Forcing air into her nose and out through her mouth, she worked to hold herself together until she could get home. As she approached the exit on the freeway, she suddenly changed her mind.

How do I explain to Heidi that my boyfriend is cheating on me? That I was stupid enough to believe I had a chance with a celebrity billionaire?

A single tear trickled down her cheek and Ivy clenched her jaw. She knew once she allowed the flood to start, it wouldn't end. Jerking on the wheel, she pulled off onto a scenic road that led to a lake.

Ivy parked in the visitor lot, grabbed a handful of cookies and began walking around the lake until she left the crowds behind. The sand turned to rocks and boulders, but she trudged on. Eventually, she climbed one of the large rocks and perched herself on top.

Sitting with her legs crossed, she stared out at the smooth water. The day was beautiful with only a few puffy clouds scattered across the sky. Gulls circled overhead, keeping an eager eye on the picnics going on below them. Boats raced in the distance, many with skiers or wakeboarders skimming the waves behind them. Children squealed as they dipped their toes into the cold water then ran back to their families, but the noise barely touched Ivy.

A dark, shadowed forest sat at her back, the wet rock beneath her and a chilly breeze caressed her cheeks, but Ivy took no notice of it. Her mind was back at the Avangarde Resort as she replayed what she had heard over and over again.

Tears trickled unheeded down Ivy's cheeks as she imagined the invitation in the woman's voice. There was no mistaking the stranger's intention when she asked to give Eli the papers, 'personally'.

After a few moments, Ivy closed her eyes and shook her head. "You're an idiot, Ivy Thompson. Eli Truman is a handsome, rich, not to mention famous man, how in the world did you think someone like you could capture him?" Her chest felt as if a thousand pound weight were sitting on it. Groaning, she leaned forward and rubbed her sternum. "And I totally fell in love with him. I let myself fall in love with a two-timing jerk who women throw themselves at him everyday." Ivy paused, then jerked upright with a gasp. "Women throw themselves at him every day."

She thought back to all the times she had seen women try to capture Eli's attention. How many times had she fielded phone calls or room requests from women who were simply trying to get Eli alone?

Ivy wiped her cheeks with her hands. Letting herself go back over the conversation one more time, she realized that she had never heard Eli answer the woman back. Her heart paused for a moment then began hammering away with renewed vigor.

"Maybe I rushed out too early. Maybe nothing happened." Ivy's optimistic personality was trying desperately to stay alive as she sniffed and grabbed her phone out of her pocket. She threw her cookies to the waiting seagulls as she pulled up Eli's name.

Are you feeling better this morning? Maybe up to doing something this afternoon?

There. That gives him a chance to tell me what happened. She bit her lips as she waited for his response. *Please. Please. Tell me the truth. Please tell me it wasn't what it looked like.*

Sorry. Something came up and I'm busy all day.

Ivy's heart plummeted. "No."

Everything all right? What can I do to help?

Nothing. Just boring business stuff.

Images of what 'boring business stuff' might entail began to sift through Ivy's mind. Her tears began to flow again and Ivy angrily wiped them away. "NO!" She shouted. "No. You don't know for sure, Ivy. Give him a chance to explain. You're an adult, you can do better than to jump to conclusions."

Drawing in a shaky breath, she gave Eli one more chance.

How about I cook you dinner then?

Not a good time, sorry.

Ivy's bottom lip trembled harder the more he pushed her away.

I can bring it to your office.

Sorry. Gotta run. Maybe another time.

Ivy dropped her phone in her lap and covered her face with her hands. Great wracking sobs tore through her as she realized this was it. Even though he hadn't spoken the exact words to break off their relationship, his texts told her everything she needed to know.

ELI SET HIS PHONE DOWN on his desk and rubbed his hands down his face with a groan.

"What was so important?" Melinda asked with a pinched expression. When Eli had shut down her little planned reunion, she had instantly become impatient and irritable. Then Ivy had texted and Eli had had to get rid of her before he could finish his conversation with Melinda.

"Nothing that concerns you," he bit back. "I want those documents on my desk by the end of the day, Melinda. Are we clear?"

Melinda folded her arms and a smug expression crossed her face. "Or what, Dear? You'll divorce me?"

Eli growled. "Quit calling me dear. We're not together any more, got that?" *How did I ever find her acerbic personality attractive? She's nothing like bright and sunny Ivy.*

"But we could be. Putting our two shares together would allow us to do so much more than we could by ourselves."

Eli felt like the pulsing vein on his forehead was going to pop right out of his skin. He stood and leaned over his desk. "You're delusional, Melinda. You have no right to that treasure. We both know the divorce was final before my brothers and I found it. And we will fight with every resource we own to keep you from it."

Melinda sniffed and examined her long, manicured nails as if she wasn't the least bit put off by his anger. "That's what you say, but the date on my paper says otherwise."

"Get out."

Melinda tilted her head and grinned. "It must have been a woman."

Eli jerked back. "What?"

"The texting. It must have been a woman." Melinda slowly stood and pursed her lips at him. "You've been very careful not to touch or respond to my advances, even though we both know you're attracted to me." Her eyes narrowed. "Where have you been hiding her? I haven't heard anything in the media about you dating."

Eli wanted to punch his fist through a wall, but he wasn't willing to give Melinda the gratification of seeing him truly lose it. "I haven't been attracted to you in years, Melinda. You cured me of that not long after we got married. As for there being another woman, my personal life is none of your business. If and when the media picks up a story like that, you can watch from afar just as you've been doing."

Melinda gasped. "How dare you!"

With a determined stride, Eli rounded his desk and grasped her upper arm. "I think it's time you left." Locking his fingers in place so she couldn't get away from him but also so he wouldn't hurt her, Eli marched her down the hall and to the front doors.

The security guards must have noticed Eli's attitude because they scrambled to open the large doors as he approached. As Eli pulled Melinda out into the sunshine, bright flashes exploded from the bottom of the steps.

"What the-?" Eli threw his hand up in front of his face. "Why the heck is the media here?"

"For this," Melinda spun towards him, wrapped her arms around his neck and kissed him on the lips.

Eli immediately grabbed Melinda and pushed her back. "What kind of dirty trick are you playing?" Pushing her back, Eli glared at the reporters and photographers shouting at him and stormed back inside.

Eli headed straight to his private restroom where he washed his face and brushed his teeth to get the smell and taste of Melinda off of him. "That woman is going to be the death of me."

"Dude, girl or no girl, I'm gonna take her out if she tries to pull something like that again." Nelson's normal happy-go-lucky tone was low and angry.

Eli leaned on the counter and let his head hang between his arms. "Saw that, did you?"

"The whole world is seeing it."

"Crap," Eli muttered. "Crap, crap, CRAP!" He slammed his hand down on the marble countertop.

"I would use a different word, but that works." Nelson folded his arms and leaned against the doorframe. "And you're sitting in a big pile of it. Just who do you think is going to see that picture as soon as it breaks?"

Eli closed his eyes and his heart sank. *This is everything I was hoping wouldn't happen.*

"Is this the time where I get to say 'I told you so'."

"I'm not in the mood, Nelson," Eli sighed, suddenly weary. *Fate must hate me.* Standing up, Eli pushed past his brother and grabbed his phone off his desk. He fired off a text.

Are you still up for doing something tonight? Eli tapped his foot as he watched his screen. Five minutes eeked by and there was no sign of a response.

Ivy, I'd really like to talk to you.

Eli rubbed the bridge of his nose. Yesterday's headache had blown into the migraine he had lied to Ivy about. "Come on, come on," he grumbled. After several more minutes, he pushed the call button.

He paced his office while the phone rang, running his fingers through his hair, until eventually the voicemail picked up. "Ivy, it's Eli. We need to talk. Call me."

Nelson stood in the doorway shaking his head.

"Got something you want to say?" Eli asked, glaring at his brother.

"I realize we need to figure out this thing with Melinda, but just for the record, when everything falls apart with Ivy, I'm on her side." Nelson marched across the room to the door that led to the hallway. "I'll wait for you at your house," he called over his shoulder.

Eli groaned and fell onto his couch. He looked hopefully at his phone, but Ivy still hadn't answered his texts. He suddenly felt every one of his thirty-four years. His body felt heavy and old. Slowly, he stood up and walked back to his desk. Pulling up his email, he searched to see if Melinda had had the papers sent over yet.

Once he found them, he quickly forwarded them to his lawyer. He glanced at his phone again. *Still no answer. That isn't like her.* Eli glanced at his watch. *Maybe I have time to run by her apartment before I meet Hayden and Nelson.*

Grabbing his jacket, Eli headed toward the back of the resort and his private parking spot. He nearly jumped out of his skin when his phone rang in his hand. He scrambled to answer it. "Ivy?"

"What? Who's Ivy?" The rough tones of Gregory Holmes, Eli's lawyer, rang through the phone speaker.

"Sorry." Eli sighed and rubbed his temple. "Did you get the email?"

"Yeah. That's why I'm calling. We should get together as soon as possible to get this figured out."

"What did you have in mind?" Eli glanced again at his watch.

"My wife just left for a girls afternoon. I can come over right now."

"I was going to-" Eli's shoulders slumped. "Nevermind. Nelson is already at my house. I can call Hay and get him there as well."

"Great. See you in fifteen."

Eli hung up and stared at his phone for a moment before trying one more time.

Please, Ivy. I really need to talk to you.

When there was no response, he shook his head and pressed the button on his keyring to unlock his car. He shot off a text to Hayden before climbing inside. Sliding into the seat, he tossed his phone in the passenger seat and pulled out of the parking lot.

Once at his house, he trudged inside.

"Don't you have any food in this house?" Nelson yelled from the kitchen.

"Groceries came yesterday," Eli grumbled. He walked over to his large, leather sofa and laid down lengthwise. His head felt like it might break into tiny splinters any moment and his anxiety over Ivy not answering his texts and calls was making it worse.

"Dude. You need to rethink how you shop. All you've got is fruits and veggies and junk. A disaster like this at least calls for some sugar. Where the heck are your cookies and brownies?"

Eli didn't answer Nelson's query. Instead, he moaned and covered his face with his hand.

Hayden burst through the door a few minutes later, Gregory on his heels.

"All right, gentlemen. Good to see you, although, I wish it was under different circumstances." Gregory stalked across the open expanse and put his briefcase on the table, quickly snapping open the latches.

"Eli, you going to join us?" Hayden called from the seat he had pulled out next to Gregory.

"I'm afraid if I stand up, my head might fall off. I'll listen from here."

Hayden grunted, but left him be.

"So what are we dealing with?" Nelson said around a mouthful of apple.

"According to the papers your brother sent me, Melinda is suing for her share of the treasure. She claims that their divorce was not final before you struck gold and according to California laws that entitles her to half of his share."

Nelson choked. "Are you kidding me? She can't do that, can she?"

"We're not in California, we're in Washington," Hayden growled.

"True," Gregory nodded. "But at that point your brother was still considered a California resident. You three were brand new to the state.

If her paperwork has any legitimacy, I will look into Washington state citizenship laws and see if they can help us."

"Have you seen the papers?"

Gregory nodded. "Yes. But I plan to send a request for the originals. Or at least a meeting to see them. She seems to be working on the fact that one of the papers has some smudged ink, making the date appear later in the year." Gregory shook his head. "It seems flimsy to me. Every document will have the date written several times, so I'm not sure how a lawyer could think one smudged date is enough. There has to be something I'm missing. Which is why I want to see the originals. All I have are scans of very specific parts of the documents."

Eli's mind churned the longer the men talked at the table. Thoughts of Ivy, Melinda's media set-up and the treasure all fought for dominance. *I wish we'd never found that blasted room.*

Slowly, the voices became more muddled and his thoughts began trailing off. The afternoon sun beating through the front window felt warm and soothing and his exhausted body gave into the pull of sleep.

Eli awoke with a jerk in full darkness. Sitting up, he looked around, finding himself alone. He scrubbed his face and glanced at his watch. "Shoot." He'd slept all day, and it was too late to speak to Ivy.

Leaning over, he turned on a lamp and spotted his phone on the coffee table. It was blinking with a message and he quickly grabbed it and turned it on, hope soaring through him.

We'll fill you in on Gregory's plan later. Thought you needed the nap.

Eli huffed. Leaving his phone on the table, he stumbled up the stairs to his bedroom and did his best to go back to sleep.

CHAPTER 19

Ivy had barely slept last night. Her conscience had eaten at her all night for ignoring Eli. When his last text came through with the word 'please' in it, she had nearly caved. She had been terrified that Eli was going to break up with her and Ivy hadn't felt like she could handle talking to him just yet.

She now sat at her tiny kitchen table, a steaming mug of tea next to her, her hair wadded into a bun on top of her head and wrapped into an old, worn robe. The mug was forgotten as she read the headline on her phone. Despite the fact that the device trembled in her shaking hands, the words were clear.

Bachelor No More. Overnight Billionaire Takes Back Ex Wife.

A brightly colored photo stood in stark contrast to the black and white print, very clearly showing Eli kissing a tall, leggy, blonde on the front steps of the castle.

The longer Ivy sat there, the more blurred the photo became. Every tiny ounce of hope she had held onto from yesterday blew into the wind like pieces of ash.

She sat frozen until a set of hands gently took her phone from her and set it face down on the table. She gasped in a sob and started shaking uncontrollably. Those same hands grabbed her arms and pulled her into a soft embrace.

"Oh, Ivy. I'm so sorry," Heidi murmured. She held Ivy until the shaking and sobs slowed down. "It's going to be okay. You're going to be okay. Maybe not today or tomorrow, but eventually, you're going to be okay." Heidi rubbed her arms over Ivy's back. "Just let yourself purge, get it out. It's all right."

Ivy had never been more grateful for her roommate. There were times when Heidi had been annoying and over the top with her fluttery personality, but right now, she was exactly what Ivy needed.

"Too bad money can't buy manners," Heidi huffed. "No amount of money gives someone the right to be a horse's hind end."

Ivy snorted out a laugh amongst her tears, but the smile quickly dropped again. "I had hoped I had misunderstood yesterday. He didn't answer her back. I thought, maybe-" Ivy stepped back, wiped her tears and gestured toward the phone. "I guess now I know what he was doing when he wasn't talking."

"Don't worry your pretty, little head about it." Heidi handed Ivy a box of tissues. "Tonight we'll gorge on cookies and ice cream and do as much bad-mouthing about men as we want. Rich, handsome men in particular."

Ivy's bottom lip trembled. "I love him, Heidi. I thought he was the one."

"Oh, Sweetie." Heidi pulled her in for another hug. "You deserve so much more than a spoiled, jerky cheater. We'll find you the perfect guy yet." Heidi leaned back. "Hey! What about Nelson? You guys get along great and he seems like a cool guy."

Ivy rolled her eyes. "Nellie is like a brother! Not to mention how weird family dinners would be."

"Yeah, okay. You're right. And there's no way I'm suggesting the scary one who uses butcher knives. So," Heidi shrugged, "we'll just have to find you a different billionaire."

Ivy laughed and wiped her face.

Both girls jumped when their doorbell rang.

"Who the heck could that be this early?" Heidi hurried over and looked through their peephole. She gasped and spun around. "It's him!" She mouthed.

Ivy's eyes widened and her heart picked up speed. "Eli?" She squeaked.

Heidi nodded.

Ivy looked down at herself and groaned. "I can't let him see me like this!"

"Hurry!" Heidi shooed Ivy toward the bedrooms. "Go change and stuff. I'll hold him off for a few minutes."

Ivy darted down the hallway, scurrying into her room and slamming the door. Leaning her ear against the hollow panel, she could hear murmured voices coming from the front room.

She put her hand over her heart, amazed it was still working after everything it had been through in the last couple of days. Suddenly, her sadness turned into anger. *How dare he come here after what he's done to me. He didn't even have the courtesy to break up with me before he got together with his ex. Why am I hiding like I'm the one who was wrong?*

Anger stiffened her spine, and she began storming through her room. She pulled out her favorite jeans and a shirt that brought out the color of her eyes and started to get dressed. "He might be breaking up with me, but that doesn't mean I have to make it comfortable for him."

ELI SHIFTED UNCOMFORTABLY on the couch as he waited for Ivy to appear. He hadn't been able to get back to sleep last night after his nap and tossed and turned as he worried about Ivy and her reaction to the media. He had hurried over as soon as he dared this morning, hoping to beat the news to her door.

Eli tugged on the collar on his shirt. By the glare Heidi was giving him over her coffee mug, he felt like he might be too late.

Eli's eyes darted around the room, eventually landing on a pile of mail on the small table next to the sofa. At first he dismissed them, but the bold, red letter 'URGENT' caught his attention. He frowned and reached for the pile, only to pull back and look at Heidi. Heidi's back was to him as she refilled her mug, so he reached out again.

There were several envelopes, all addressed to Ivy and Eli felt a moment of panic. Glancing at the return addressed, he noticed they were all medical bills. *Is she sick?* His mind spun until he discovered the last envelope was addressed to a 'Ms. Augusta Thompson' and marked with the stamp 'DUE NOW'.

Eli's heart fell to his stomach. *Bills. They're all medical bills for Ivy's mom.* He counted the mail. *There must be half a dozen of them. Just how far in debt is she? And why didn't she tell me?*

"Can I help you?" Ivy's normally honey warm tones were gone. In their place was a coldness Eli had never heard before and it made him wince to think of how much she must be hurting to speak like that.

"Ivy," he said in a calm voice. "I need to speak to you. Something happ-"

Ivy put up her hand. "I know. I was there."

Eli stilled. "What do you mean you were there? There, where?"

Ivy's green eyes seemed extra large this morning and practically glowed against the green shirt she was wearing. Her hair was pulled back in a neat bun, but a couple of loose tendrils floated around her face. She had dark circles under her eyes and her normally pale skin was positively ghostly this morning. Eli's fingers twitched with the desire to reach out and his chest ached with the need to hold her. However, her glare and clenched fists let him know his advances would not be welcome.

Ivy pinched her lips for a moment before straightening her shoulders and sticking her chin up. "I decided to surprise you with some cookies yesterday, so I headed over to your house, expecting you to be nursing a headache."

Eli felt his nostrils flare, and heat crept up his neck as he heard the accusation in her tone. *How did everything get so out of hand?*

"Surprise!" Ivy tilted her head. "Your housekeeper informed me you were at the office. So, I thought I'd bring you the treat there. Imagine my second surprise when I approached your office only to hear you talking with a woman."

Eli felt his temperature spike. The frustration he had been dealing with since Melinda slipped back into his life began to break free. "Are you saying you stood outside my door and eavesdropped, then? I would have thought you knew better to believe things you don't have the context of," he snapped.

"Funny thing." Ivy stood straighter and stepped toward him. "I told myself the same thing. After I heard her proposition you, I hightailed it out of there only to force myself to pause and think. I didn't have all the facts, surely I had misunderstood. There was no way I would fall in love with a man who would cheat on me like that."

Eli felt as if he had been dealt a physical blow. *She loves me?*

Ignoring his shock, Ivy plowed ahead. "So, I tried to give you the benefit of the doubt. I texted you, trying to give you the chance to come clean, to tell me what was going on. And you know what I got?" She answered her own question before Eli could open his mouth. "I got kicked to the curb. Your texts made it all too obvious you wanted me out of the way. So, I got out of the way. Happy now?"

"No, I'm not happy! You don't under-"

"You LIED to me, Eli!" Tears started trickling down her cheeks. "Flat out lied. But even after that, I woke up this morning planning to let you explain everything. Maybe somehow," she laughed harshly and pushed her fingers into her hair, "somehow I still misunderstood. But then," she stopped her pacing and looked him in the eye, "I woke up to see you plastered all over the media kissing your ex-wife. No wonder you wanted me out of your hair so badly yesterday. You should have just told me the truth."

Eli's breathing had picked up during her rant and the anger that had been building for several days finally broke through his dam of self control. Rather than defend himself he struck back. "You want the truth?

That's rich coming from someone who has lied to me since the beginning of our relationship, if you can even call it that."

Ivy reared back as if she had been slapped and the blood drained from her face. "What are you talking about?" She said quietly.

Eli stalked toward her, towering over her small frame, his chest heaving with every breath. "You played the part so well. I'll admit you had me fooled. I thought you were different from all the other women. I thought it wasn't all about the money to you. You didn't want to eat at the fancy restaurants, you were worried about bringing me home to your garage sale couch, but it was all just an act."

Ivy pushed against his chest, creating a little distance between them. "I haven't been acting at all!"

Eli took one giant step over to the stack of bills. Clenching them in his fist, he waved them in her face. He felt a warning ping in his conscience, but he shoved it aside. "When did you plan to ask me to pay your bills, huh? Or were you just hoping I would start buying you expensive gifts so you could trade them in for the cash?" His tirade ended abruptly when her eyes filled with tears. The sight of her sadness tore right through him.

Her full, bottom lip trembled and the trickle of tears turned into a flood. When she spoke, her voice was quiet but strong. "I didn't tell you about them because I didn't want you to think I was with you for your money. Truth is, I'm in debt up to my eyeballs. It's why I haven't gone to college yet. My mom was sick for years and I was the only person who was around to take care of her. I almost didn't make it out of high school because of how much time it took to care for her on top of holding down a job so we could eat. She lasted three years after graduation and when she died, all the bills went to me, her adult daughter. Since I'm only making minimum payments, I'll be paying off her debt for years. And some of the companies," she nodded toward his fist, "as you can see, are getting anxious. I came out here to make a fresh start, to get away from the eyes in my small town who watched me with pity everywhere I went. I was so sick of being a charity case." She shook her head and stepped back. "I had no idea I would meet you or fall for you. I'm sorry I kept it hidden from you, but you were already so hounded by gold diggers that I thought it better to just keep my financial troubles out of our relationship completely." She took another step back. "I guess it doesn't matter now. I hope you're happy with your wife." Then she disappeared into her room.

Eli stood stunned at her story. He wanted to yell, to tell her he knew she was simply using him, but the sincerity in her face and voice couldn't be disputed. *Nelson warned me. He told me I hadn't truly paid attention.*

"I think you need to leave," Heidi's harsh tone woke him from his thoughts.

Eli clenched his jaw, but knew there was no point in arguing. He had messed up beyond repair this time. With a short nod, he dropped the papers on the couch and dragged himself out the door. His feet felt like lead and he had the distinct feeling that he had left something valuable behind.

While driving back to the resort, Eli's phone rang, and he pressed the bluetooth button. "Yes?" He snapped.

"Whoa. Don't kill the messenger," Hayden muttered across the line.

Eli sighed and gripped the steering wheel tighter. "Sorry. What do you need, Hayden?"

"Gregory wants to meet again. Says he has good news."

At least something is going right. "Today's Sunday. I didn't realize lawyers work on Sundays."

"Perks of being a billionaire, I guess."

Right. It always comes back to the money. "Be there in ten."

CHAPTER 20

The next couple of weeks flew by in a haze for Eli and his brothers. Gregory had found a flaw in Melinda's suit almost immediately, but it had taken several days to get into court and eventually get the case thrown out. Then, the media had descended yet again and refused to leave Eli alone.

He had buried himself at his house, not even travelling back and forth to his office in the castle, as he waited for the paparazzi storm to die down. During his alone time, he had spent most of it thinking about Ivy. After backing away from the situation, it had been easy to see her point of view and forgive her holding back the fact that she was in struggling financially. His heart ached as he thought about all she had taken on at such a young age. *And yet she still smiles and spreads happiness everywhere she goes.* He sighed. *I miss her.* He thought as he tied his tie at the bathroom mirror. *More than I ever thought possible.* His shoulders drooped. "I love her," he said to his reflection. He shook his head. *How did I not see it before?*

Everything about her drew him in. Not only was he attracted to her red hair and full lips, but to her genuine kindness and optimistic attitude. "She had every right to nail me to the wall when everything blew up, but instead she told me to be happy. Yes, she kept something back from me, but now that I know, I understand why she did it. There's no way she's a golddigger, it's just not in her nature." He adjusted his cufflinks. "I don't deserve her, but I want her anyway."

Today, he was finally headed in to work and he was more than a little anxious to speak to her. His mind swam with dozens of ways to say he was sorry. The normal flowers and chocolates seemed too trite.

"It needs to be bigger than that. Something that will help her trust me again. But what?"

He still hadn't decided on a course of action by the time he pulled into his private parking stall at the back of the castle. He slipped in the side door and headed toward his office, but couldn't bring himself to go inside. *I have to see her.* Instead of turning into his doorway, he kept walking straight and headed toward the lobby.

People scurried in and out, some at the front desk, some in the lounge area, but nowhere did he see the woman he loved. Frowning, he walked across the floor to the counter.

"May I- Mr. Truman!" A dark headed, middle-aged woman jerked when she realized who was standing before her. "H-how may I help you, Sir?"

"I'd like to speak to Ms. Thompson," Eli said quietly. He glanced around and noticed quite a few people were watching him. *Don't they have anything better to do?*

The woman, whose name tag said 'Janet', cleared her throat and wrung her hands. "She's not here, I'm afraid."

Eli's head snapped back toward her. "What do you mean she's not here? She always works this shift."

Janet squared her shoulders and put up her chin. "Just like I said, she's not here."

"Well, where is she?" He demanded, leaning over the counter.

"I don't know."

"You don't know?" Eli raised an eyebrow.

"Nope." Janet folded her arms and cocked a hip.

"You've got a lot of nerve coming out here and asking for Ivy," a masculine voice said from his right side.

"Denton," Janet warned.

Eli looked the security guard in the eye. *Oh yeah, this is the guy that was flirting with Ivy.* "I don't know what you're so upset about, but I need to speak to Ivy." Eli pulled himself up to his full height. *I'm not going to let this little punk get in my way.*

"Yeah, well, she doesn't want to talk to you."

Eli narrowed his eyes. "How do you know?"

Denton folded his arms, not the least bit put out by Eli's attitude. "Pretty sure she quit just so she wouldn't have to talk to you."

Eli jerked back. "She quit!" He shouted, then immediately ducked his head and pulled his voice back down. "When did she quit?"

Denton rolled his eyes. "Two weeks ago. I'll let you guess why." With a sneer, Denton turned and went back to his station at the door.

Eli ignored Denton's attitude. *I don't have time to deal with him right now.* Breaking into a jog, he hurried back to the hallway and straight out the door to his car. Throwing it into gear, he peeled out of the parking lot and sped to her apartment.

A nervous sweat trickled down his back when he arrived and jumped out of the car. Yanking off his suit coat, he threw it in the backseat, not caring whether it got wrinkled. He bounded up the steps to Ivy's apartment two at a time and pounded on her door.

"Come on, come on," he muttered before pounding again.

"What in this world- Oh. It's you." Heidi shook her head and went to close the door, but Eli threw his hand against it.

"Where's Ivy?"

Heidi huffed and folded her arms across her chest. "Wouldn't you like to know?"

Eli cursed in his head. "Yes. I would. I have something important to tell her."

"I think you said enough." Heidi tried to close the door again, but Eli was stronger.

"Where is she?" He asked louder.

"Shh!" Heidi put her finger over her lips. "You're gonna bring my landlady up here and then we'll both be in trouble."

"Just tell me where she is, then!" Eli raised his eyebrows.

Heidi sighed. "She's not here. She moved out."

"What?" Eli's jaw fell slack, and he felt as if he had been socked in the gut with a brick.

"Said she couldn't stand to stick around someone who thought so little of her, so she headed out." Heidi narrowed her eyes. "Naive as she was, that girl loved you and you threw it back in her face. If I wasn't already concerned about the state of your brain, I'd knock your lights out. But I'm afraid I'd do more damage to it than there already is."

Eli dropped his arm from the door. *Gone. She's truly gone.* Ignoring Heidi's insult he choked out, "Do you- do you know where she went?"

"No." Heidi said sharply. "And even if I did, I wouldn't tell you. She didn't really know herself when she left. She just said she couldn't stay, packed up her car and left."

When Eli didn't speak again, Heidi slammed the door in his face.

Eli felt numb as he walked back down the stairs to his car and pulled out. He blinked when he parked back at the resort, having no memory of the drive back. His shoulders drooped as he walked back to his office and slumped into his chair.

A knock came at the door.

"I'm busy," Eli called out, burying his face in his hands. *What do I do now? She's gone. I didn't realize-*

"I'm guessing you finally tried to find Ivy," Nelson said from the doorway.

Eli didn't look up. "I think that's the first time you've ever knocked on my door. Usually you just burst in."

Nelson shrugged. "Yeah, well, you didn't look like you would appreciate me doing that."

"True enough," Eli mumbled. He heard a squeak as Nelson settled on the couch.

"So, what are you going to do about it?"

Eli finally looked up. "About what?"

Nelson rolled his eyes. "Are you freakin' kidding me right now? How dumb are you, Eli? Aren't you going to fight for her at all?"

"Just what do you expect me to do about it, huh? She left. No notice, no goodbye. She stopped taking my calls before everything even went down. So, please tell me, O Wise One, how I am expected to fight for her."

Nelson folded his arms and looked smug. "If you'd look beyond yourself for one moment, you might find you have a secret weapon in your corner."

Eli froze, then slowly straightened. "You know where she is," he breathed.

Nelson tilted his head from side to side. "I might. See, one of us wasn't stupid enough to accuse her of being a golddigger."

Eli winced. "She told you about that?"

Nelson nodded. "Pretty sure she told me everything while she bawled her eyes out over her mug of hot chocolate."

Eli shrunk into himself. "Yeah, that wasn't my finest moment."

Nelson snorted but didn't speak.

Eli glanced up. "Do I have any chance with her at all?"

Nelson narrowed his eyes. "Why do you want one? You made it clear what you thought of her before she left. Why do you want to speak to her now?"

Eli scrubbed his hands down his face and sighed. "Because I love her," he said softly.

"What was that?" Nelson put his hand behind his ear and turned it toward Eli.

"Because I love her! I haven't been able to breathe properly these past two weeks! Now that everything with Melinda is over I want my life back. I want Ivy back. Everything reminds me of her. Of her kindness, her smile, her laugh." Eli put a fist to his chest. "I ache to-"

"Hold it right there!" Nelson put his hand up. "I don't want the gushy details."

Eli slumped back in his chair, rubbing his heart absentmindedly. "Will you help me get her back?"

Nelson laughed. "Uh, no."

Eli's stomach fell.

"Wooing her is up to you, but I will help you have the chance."

Eli jumped up. "Great! Where is she?"

"Whoa, there, Cowboy. I think you need to take a minute to think of a plan. You didn't just break Ivy's heart, you obliterated it. You can't just run in and say sorry. That isn't enough."

Eli dropped back down. Feeling strangled, he tugged off his tie and threw it across the room. "So, what do you suggest?"

Nelson rubbed his hands and grinned.

Ah, crud. What did I get myself into? Eli grimaced.

CHAPTER 21

I vy closed her eyes and rolled her neck, trying desperately to work out the kinks in her shoulders.

"Hey, Sunshine! Table three's ready!" Ben, the head cook, yelled from behind the counter.

"On it!" Ivy pasted a smile on and walked over to get the plates. Her waitressing job at the small cafe wasn't glamorous, nor did it pay nearly as well as her job at the resort had, but it was all she had been able to find in the small college town she had chosen.

Ever since she had run away from Avangarde Castle, she had been trying to figure out what to do with her life. One or two online college classes a year wasn't getting her anywhere, and she was getting behind in her mother's bills. She had finally decided that getting an education, even if it put her in more debt for a time, was the only way she was eventually going to bring in more money. So, she had contacted an agency who would help her consolidate her debts and set up a payment plan with the collectors. Then she had gone to the community college and set up an appointment to talk to a counselor about financial aid.

I might be in debt a bit longer than I would like, but hopefully in the end it will be for the best.

"Hey, Ives? I have an emergency, can you take the plates to table nine?" Suzy shook her phone and scrunched up her face.

"Sure," Ivy said with that same fake smile fixed into place. "No worries."

"Thanks." Suzy hurried through the back of the restaurant.

With a deep breath, Ivy collected the two plates and walked over. "Here we go," she chirped. "Who had the fish and chips?" She looked up and nearly dropped the plates. "Eli," she gasped.

175

The crushing pain that had become her constant companion ever since their fight two weeks ago, came back with a vengeance.

"Whoa, there." Nelson reached out and grabbed the two plates before they could fall and set them on the table. "Thanks, Ivy. I'm starving."

Ivy turned her water filled eyes on Nelson and pinched her lips together. "How could you?" She whispered hoarsely.

Nelson's face softened. "Give him a chance."

Ivy shook her head and spun on her heel. *I can't do it. I'm not ready to pretend I don't care.*

"Ivy!" Eli's deep voice rang through the room as she ran.

Ivy darted out the back door and into a dark alley with a dumpster. She bent over and rested her hands on her knees, gulping in air and praying she wouldn't throw up.

"Ivy," Eli's voice came from behind her.

She whipped around and backed up. "What do you want, Mr. Truman?" She snapped.

Eli winced and a small part of Ivy was glad. *Good. Let him hurt for a minute.* Immediately, her conscience kicked in and she felt bad for reacting like she did "I'm sorry." She rubbed her forehead. "I shouldn't have spoken like that." She straightened her shoulders and put her chin in the air. Her hands were clenched together in an effort to keep from trembling and she held them against her stomach. "What is it you needed?" She forced her voice to stay calm and cool.

Eli studied her for a moment. There was no mistaking the sorrow written across his face. His eyebrows were downturned as well as the edges of his mouth. His shoulders were low and for once, he didn't look like the billionaire in charge. "You, Ivy. I need you."

Ivy's eyes widened, and she choked on air. "What did you say?"

"Ivy!" Ben stuck his head out the back door. "What are you doing? You're on the clock, do this stuff on your own time, we've got work to do." He glared at Eli before looking back at Ivy and jerking his head toward the inside of the building.

"Excuse me," Ivy murmured as she took a couple of steps toward the door.

"I'm not letting you go, Ivy," Eli murmured as she passed him.

"You already did," she said before disappearing inside.

Ivy felt numb for the rest of her shift. She went through the motions on auto-pilot and managed to not spill any trays by the time the cafe closed up.

While she lay in bed later that night, her mind whirled. She stared at the ceiling with her hands folded across her stomach. *Why did he come? What did he mean he wants me? Didn't he already make it clear he doesn't want me? Maybe things didn't work out with his ex.* The thought that he had only come crawling back because his ex wife left again caused Ivy to curl into a ball to stop the pain. She forced herself to breathe slowly and inch by inch the tension drained from her body. Once she was able to lay flat again, she was damp and exhausted from the emotional upheaval.

Rolling onto her side, she pulled her blanket up to her chin and tucked her hands under her pillow. "Doesn't matter, Ivy. You're strong enough to get through this. You've done hard things before. You can do hard things again. Odds are he won't try and contact you again, anyway."

ELI STARED AT THE CEILING of the hotel room while Nelson snored away in the other bed. *She looked so broken. What have I done? How can I get her to talk to me? Is it too late? Is there any hope? Will she believe me if I say I love her?*

His mind was a melting pot of emotions and questions and he knew he would never get to sleep that night. Instead of trying to fight it, he welcomed the uncertainty and the hurt. *It's no more than you deserve.*

"But how do I fix it?" He whispered to the darkness.

Nelson snorted and rolled over. Eli waited until his brother's breathing regulated again before continuing his personal dialogue. "What would show her that I know I was wrong?"

"Dude, I told you you couldn't just show up and say sorry," Nelson mumbled.

"But what *can* I do? She doesn't even want to speak to me."

"Maybe you need to outlast her hurt," he grumbled. "Show her she can trust you."

Eli blinked a few times, ruminating on the thought. "Yeah, maybe," he whispered.

CHAPTER 22

"Hey, Ben," Ivy said as she tied her apron around her waist.

"Hey, yourself." Ben stopped flipping burgers and raised his eyebrows. "You okay?"

Ivy put the necessary smile on her face. "Just fine, thanks," she lied. Despite her best intentions, all day a small part of her had been waiting for Eli to call or text or do... something! *It was just a fluke. Last night was a fluke. He probably just felt bad about how things went down and was trying to ease his conscience.*

"Okay, well, hop to it then. Table ten is ready for their plates."

"On it." She did her best to inject some enthusiasm into her tone, but from Ben's expression, she wasn't sure it worked.

At least I'm not crying anymore. Ben probably wouldn't know what to do with that. When she had gotten this job, Ivy had learned the fine art of shoving emotions so far back that she become numb inside. Her chest felt like a hollow cavity that was missing the most important part of her. *Huh. I guess Eli and I finally have something in common.*

Holding the two plates in her hands, Ivy took a deep breath and stepped into the noisy dining room. Table ten was around the corner to the left and she weaved her way toward it. Her steps slowed when she spotted two heads of dark hair at her destination. *Oh no.*

Nelson spotted her first and grinned wide. "Ivy! Long time no see."

Forgetting all pretense, Ivy plunked their plates on the table. "Is there anything else you need?"

She kept her eyes on Nelson, refusing to look at Eli. *I can't. I just can't.*

"I'm good, what about you?" Nelson turned the question to his brother.

Ivy closed her eyes, clenched her jaw and forced herself to look. Dark circles were under his eyes, testifying of a sleepless night. His hair was rumpled, and he had a thick stubble on his beautiful face. Ivy's fingers itched with the desire to trace his cheekbones and feel the beard against her skin. But she clenched her hands into fists and ignored the urge.

His grey eyes appeared sad and weary. Ivy scoffed internally. *He called you a golddigger. He doesn't feel bad, it's your imagination.*

"Oh, I need something, Nelson," Eli answered, but his eyes never left Ivy. "You see, I lost something precious and I won't give up until I get it back."

A tremor ran down Ivy's spine and she stiffened her shoulders.

"Huh. That stinks. Dinner looks good though." Nelson picked up his burger and took a large bite.

"Good luck with that," Ivy shot back before leaving. *Numb. You are numb. You don't have a heart left to hurt, Ivy Thompson. Don't listen to him.*

ELI SLUMPED IN HIS seat. What little energy he had, had been used when he spoke to Ivy. *She looks so small and fragile. You did that to her. Three times you chewed her up and spit her out and now you dare to ask her to forgive you again?* Eli shook his head. "I don't have the right."

Nelson wiped his mouth with a napkin. "What was that?"

"I don't have the right to ask for her forgiveness." Eli pulled his eyes up to Nelson's. "She hates me and rightfully so. I should just leave her be."

"This." Nelson pointed a finger. "This is exactly what she thinks of you. Every time something gets tough, you back off. You've done it throughout your whole relationship. You're proving her right."

"She won't talk to me, Nelson!" Eli hissed. "I can't force her to forgive me."

"No, but you can show you're not going anywhere. Come back here every night until she talks to you, no matter how long it takes. Show her she's more important than anything else. Your words aren't going to be enough. In fact, your words are what got you here in the first place. You're going to have to show her."

Eli sat straight and looked at his brother. "When did you become such an expert on love?"

Nelson grinned. "And you all thought those teenage magazines were a waste of time." He took another large bite.

Eli's eyebrows jumped. "I knew it! I knew you were still reading them!"

Nelson rolled his eyes. "It was *one* time! One time, Dude." Nelson leaned in close. "But believe me, one time through one of those magazines is all it takes. It's like a woman encyclopedia. Not to mention you can't unsee some of that stuff." He gave a fake shiver.

Eli shook his head. His eyes drifted from the table to the beautiful, but sad waitress making her way around the tables. *He's right. I just need to prove myself.* A couple of ideas popped into his head. "Nelson." He turned back to look across the booth. "I've got an idea."

"Finally! I was beginning to think I was the only one with any brains on this mission."

Eli shook his head and picked up his fork. "Tomorrow morning, we have work to do."

CHAPTER 23

I vy braced herself. For the last five nights she had been forced to serve Eli and Nelson with a smile on her face. *How in the world are they staying away from the resort for so long? Eli has to be going nuts. And who is running Nelson's camping trips?*

Locking her car, she got out and headed into the cafe. *Maybe I should listen to what he has to say. I mean, this can't go on forever, can it? What would he do if I never spoke to him?*

A loud voice could be heard bellowing in the kitchen and Ivy frowned. "What happened? Ben never yells like that." She stepped in the side door, hung up her jacket and grabbed an apron.

"I wouldn't serve that garbage to my pig, let alone a human being! I should make you eat this first and we'll see how you like it!"

"Hayden!" Ivy gasped as she walked around the corner.

Hayden spun and his scowl turned into a smile. "Ivy! Been awhile."

"W-what are you doing here?" Her heart began to thump painfully in her chest. *What is going on?*

"Doing my best to whip these...," Hayden looked disdainfully over his shoulder and back, "ingrates into shape. Not a one of them knows the difference between poached and hard boiled."

Ivy tisked her tongue. "Be nice, Hayden. Not everyone goes to culinary school."

Hayden rolled his eyes. "Speaking of school. You need to go to the manager's office."

"The manager's office?" She squeaked. "Why? And what does that have to do with school?"

Hayden pasted on an innocent look. "I don't know what you're talking about. I was only told to give you a message."

Panic immediately enveloped her. "Who's in that office, Hayden?"

"Guess you'll find out." Hayden turned back and began barking orders at the workers in the kitchen.

Ivy gulped and walked across the kitchen to the far corner where the offices were. Her knock was soft, and she wasn't sure if anyone would hear it, but her fist was shaking too hard to be any louder.

"Come in."

Ivy closed her eyes as she recognized the voice. *Eli. What is he doing here?*

The door opened and Ivy stepped back. "Ivy," Eli breathed. He cleared his throat. "Come in, please." He had shaved and put on one of his power suits. His powerful persona was too big for the small office and Ivy felt as if she was choking as she stepped inside.

"What's going on?" She walked in just enough to let him shut the door.

"Have a seat." He swept his arm toward one of the old, vinyl chairs located near a desk.

"No thanks, I'd rather stand." Ivy folded her arms and leaned against the wall.

"That's fine." Eli came and stood in front of her, tugging on his collar. "Thank you for coming in."

"I didn't know it would be you in here," Ivy said curtly. "Speaking of which. What are you doing in here? And why is Hayden in the kitchen?"

Rather than answering her questions, Eli stared at her with his hands stuffed in his pockets. The longer the silence the more uncomfortable Ivy became. *What is going on? What does he want?* The feelings of betrayal and hurt that she had been shoving down for weeks were bubbling to the surface and she was ready to scream. Just as she opened her mouth to let him have it, he spoke.

"You are so beautiful," he said softly.

"What do you- what?" She sputtered. Her folded arms fell to her sides, and she had to stiffen her knees. "What are you talking about?"

Eli took a couple of steps forward. "I bought the cafe."

Her eyes went wide. "You *bought* the cafe? Whatever for? Why the heck would you do that?"

Several breaths passed before he answered. "I will do anything it takes to get you to talk to me. I figured you'd be more receptive if I called you in as your boss, rather than as myself."

Her cheeks flushed, and she shoved off the wall. "Why is it so important that we talk? I have no doubt that we said everything that needed to be said back at my apartment." She slashed a hand through the air. "Why are you bothering with this? I can just quit, you know, then you won't be my boss."

Eli's shoulders slumped and his eyes were so sad that Ivy had a hard time holding onto her anger. Her desire to soothe and comfort was nearly overwhelming. *He doesn't get to be the sad one. He's the one that betrayed me.*

"I'd just buy wherever you went next."

Ivy jerked back. "You'd what?"

"I'd just follow wherever you went until you talked to me. I'll buy as many businesses as I have to until you give me a chance." Eli raised his chin and firmed his shoulders. "You ask why?" He took another step forward. "Because you're worth it, Ivy. You're worth fighting for. You're worth chasing. You're worth holding on to. And if I have to spend my whole fortune buying up businesses, you're worth losing every penny over."

Tears began trickling down her cheeks. "But you said I was a lying, gold digger."

Eli shook his head and took another step forward. "I was wrong. I had been holding in my emotions for too long and I said things I didn't mean. I'm sorry."

"I'm still in debt."

"Not any more. I took care of it." He stepped into her personal bubble. His hand raised to her cheek where he paused before touching her. His fist clenched and unclenched as he debated his next move.

Half of Ivy was screaming for him to touch her and the other half wanted him to leave her alone. When his thumb brushed the tears from her cheek, she closed her eyes and told the negative voice to shut up. His touch sent warmth and electricity singing through her veins and for the first time in several weeks, Ivy felt alive.

"You can't just take care of it, Eli," she whispered through her tears. "I don't want your money."

"That's exactly why I did it."

Ivy's eyes shot open, and she shook her head. "What?"

Eli bracketed her face with his hands. "I know you don't want my money, and I hoped that by giving it to you, you would see that I trust that. I trust you."

Ivy's breath broke on a sob and she wrapped her arms around his midsection. "What changed your mind?"

Eli leaned down and rested his forehead against hers with a sigh. "I never truly thought you a were a gold digger to begin with. I was just mad and said some things in the heat of the moment that I shouldn't have." He leaned back. "Can you ever forgive me? Everything had come crashing down that weekend and I took it out on you. I can't even express how sorry I am."

Ivy chewed her lip and brushed the tears from her face. After a few moments she looked him in the eye. "You hurt me, Eli. How do I know I can trust you again?"

"You don't. That's the problem." He sighed, stepped away from her and pushed his hands into his hair. "Truth is, knowing me, I'll probably do something stupid sooner or later and hurt you again." He gave a harsh laugh. "I don't deserve your forgiveness, Ivy. I know I don't." He took a quick step and brought her face to his. "But I'm asking because I love you. Because I don't know how to live without you. You hold a piece of me that no one else ever has before and I don't want it back, I want you back. The only way for me to feel whole again is with you by my side. And if you'll let me, I'll spend the rest of my days trying to make up for what I've done."

Ivy's face scrunched up involuntarily and she knew she was 'ugly crying'. *Ugh. My face is probably mottled and red. Not exactly how I pictured this.* "You love me? Really?"

"Yes," he said in a husky tone. "I love everything about you. Your smile, your bubbly personality, how you sing when you say thank you-"

Ivy laughed lightly.

"I love your red hair and your eyes that seem to glow. I love how you make everyone happy, even when they don't want to be."

"You don't want to be happy?"

He rubbed his nose up and down her cheek. "I didn't think so. I thought I was content in my small, self controlled bubble. But you showed me it wasn't enough. You showed me there was more to life than work."

His words were being murmured against Ivy's skin and she thought she might melt at the riot of sensations his lips were creating. The longer he spoke, the faster her heart raced. Not from anger and hurt, but anticipation and desire.

"But do you want to know what part I love best?"

Ivy's tongue was stuck. No matter how many times she tried to swallow, there was no moisture in her mouth, it might as well have been the Sahara desert. So rather than risk sounding like an idiot, she simply nodded.

He slid his lips along her cheek until he came to the edge of her mouth. "Ever since the first time I saw you, standing in front of my office like my own personal garden fairy, I have dreamed about these lips. They have been the cause of many nights of sweet torture, especially after I finally learned what they tasted like." He left a light kiss at each corner. "Please don't take them away from me again, Ivy. I don't think I'll make it."

Ivy couldn't help the smile that crossed her face. "So now the truth comes out. You just want me for my oversized lips. I've always thought they were too big for my face."

"No. They're perfect. Just like you." The tension in the air crackled and sparked as Eli's mouth finally met hers.

Ivy hummed in contentment and reached out to pull him closer. His arms slid around her back and tucked her in as tight as she could go. One of his hand worked its way back up and tugged the rubberband out of her hair, loosing a riot of waves and he broke the kiss to bury his head in it. "You still smell like sunshine and flowers," he said huskily. "How do you do it?"

"I have no idea, but if you don't get back here," she pointed to her lips, "I'm gonna have the idea to walk out."

"Yes, Boss," he chuckled. "Whatever you say, Boss." He peppered kisses around her face. "I'm yours to command, Boss."

"You know," Ivy mused in between kisses, "You never did tell me what happened that weekend."

Eli paused. *Just do it. It's time she knew it all.* "Melinda, my ex, came back. She was trying to get part of the treasure."

Ivy's head jerked up. "What?"

Eli nodded. "Yeah. It was crazy. She had a paper from our separation that she claimed proved our divorce wasn't final when the boys and I found everything. Since we were from California, she thought she could use the community law to get half of my money."

"But I heard her proposition you! And you kissed her!"

"I know," Eli kissed her forehead. "But what you didn't hear was me telling her to get lost. And the picture was a set up. Melinda knew her case was weak, so she thought if she got back together with me, I would give her the money without a fight. She set everything up with the media so they would capture just the right moment."

Ivy buried her face in his chest. "And I fell for it, hook, line and sinker. How can she do that? Wait," she looked up again. "She's not getting any money is she?"

"No," Eli chuckled. "My lawyer found a flaw almost immediately, so she never really had a leg to stand on. Plus, Washington state residency laws say that if you buy a property with the intent to live in it, that technically makes you a resident. So, even if she had gotten to court with the date thing, Washington state doesn't have the same sharing laws as California."

"Humph. She doesn't deserve any of your money. Conniving little windbag."

Eli laughed. "Yeah, well, her lawyer boyfriend was kind of egging her on. So, she probably had no idea their case was so faulty."

"She had a boyfriend but was trying to get back together with you? What kind of woman does that?" Ivy shook her head and sniffled. "Can you forgive me for calling you liar?"

Eli shook his head. "There's nothing to forgive. You were right. I was a liar. I was trying to take care of everything without getting you involved. I thought if you knew Melinda was back in town that it would hurt you, so I did something horrible that ended up hurting you even more."

Ivy frowned up at him. "Why would you feel the need to hide everything from me? I'm a big girl. I would have believed you."

"I know. I'm sorry I didn't trust you. I just-," he sighed, "I haven't trusted a woman in a long time. And then when you were upset I lashed back at you instead of just explaining. I guess when you bottle things up for too long, they eventually explode. Nelson has been telling me that for years."

Ivy gave a sad smile. "Nelson. I want to hate him, but I'm kind of grateful. Without him, I'm pretty sure we'd have never gone out in the first place."

Eli laughed and kissed her nose. "I'd like to say that I eventually would have wised up, but truthfully, I'm not sure I would have." He dropped his voice to a conspiratorial whisper. "But don't tell him that. Nelson has a big enough head as it is."

Ivy giggled then sobered. "Can you forgive me for not telling you about my mom and everything? Once we got to know each other, I should have told you."

"I understand why you didn't say anything, and I'm not worried about it," Eli said with a smile as he went back to covering her skin with kisses.

Ivy giggled as she closed her eyes and enjoyed his ministrations. "Eli," she finally said. When he didn't stop, she reached up and grabbed his face, forcing him to look her in the eye. "Eli, I want you to know I forgive you. I love you too much not to. Yes, you hurt me, but I get that we all make mistakes. I've made plenty of them myself and if you're willing to forgive me, then I want us to move on. I've learned all too well that holding onto pain only drags us down." She shook her head. "I don't want to keep living like that."

"I don't deserve you," he whispered.

"Nor I you, but here we are. What are we going to do about it?"

"I say you come home with me where you belong and we live happily ever after. But this first," Eli mumbled right before covering her mouth with his own.

Ivy immediately threw her arms around Eli's neck to hold herself up. *How can anything in life be this wonderful?* Fireworks were exploding behind her eyelids and her legs had lost all muscle, so she tightened her grip and hung on for the ride.

ELI PUSHED ONE HAND into Ivy's silky hair and used the other to pull her body into his. He couldn't believe she was willing to forgive him. He had several other plans up his sleeve if she had turned him away. *Now that I have her, I'm never letting her go again.*

As he held her and tasted her, he knew life would never be the same. And he didn't want it to be. But before he could push forward with the future he so desperately wanted, he had to do things the right way.

Pulling back just enough so he could speak, Eli said the magic words. "Ivy Thompson, my life hasn't been the same since you walked into my office last year. You are everything I am not. Full of happiness and sunshine and you brought light back to my dreary, self imposed exile." He let his lips skim along her skin as he spoke. "Would you please marry me so that I can keep basking in your sunshine, forever?"

Ivy gasped. "You really meant forever? When you said it before I thought you were just being dramatic."

"Oh, I meant it. I even brought in the whole crew to help sweet talk you. Hayden was going to help ply you with sugar, if he ever stops yelling in the kitchen, and Nelson is doing your waitressing job so I could keep you in here and spend as much time as I needed to convince you."

Ivy's eyes got big. "Nelson is acting as a waiter? How many dishes has he broken?"

"None." Eli frowned. "That I know of."

Ivy shook her head and put her hands on either side of his face. "Are you sure you want to take on an over-aged college student who only recently got out of debt?"

"It would be my greatest pleasure," Eli smiled.

"And it would be mine to accept." Ivy tugged him down and showed him exactly how she felt.

The longer they kissed, the more a feeling of urgency built up inside of Eli. "Now," he murmured against her mouth, "let's do it now."

Ivy leaned back. "What? Are you crazy?"

Eli leaned his forehead against hers. "Crazy for you. I've held onto my rigid self control for too long. I don't want to wait to make you mine. Let's jump in the plane and fly to Vegas."

Ivy's jaw dropped. "You can't be serious."

"I'm totally serious. Do you really want to go through the media storm when they catch wind of our engagement? It'll take us a year of planning just to appease them. Of course, if you want a big wedding I'll wait. Do you... want a big one?" He winced as if waiting for a hard blow.

Ivy smiled. "No. I've never imagined myself as having a big wedding. You, me and a few close family members would have been all I wanted anyway, but you're right. Waiting for that long isn't worth it for me. I'd rather have you now."

Eli gave her a fierce kiss then grabbed her hand. Sneaking out of the office, they headed straight for the parking lot. It took no time at all to jump in his car and hit the highway.

"What about Nelson and Hayden?" Ivy cried as they left the restaurant in the distance.

"Eh, they're big boys. One of them will figure it out." He reached over and grabbed Ivy's hand. Now that he had her back, he didn't want to let her go even for a second. Her touch healed his broken parts, and he wasn't about to wait to have her just so they could plan a massive wedding neither of them wanted.

Ivy squealed and bounced in her seat. "I can't believe we're doing this! Wait." Her eyes got wide, and she looked over at him. "Did you say jump in *the* plane? As in you have your own plane?" Her voice shot up an octave as she spoke.

"Uh, yeah, billionaire, remember? Despite the mess with the media, there are definitely some perks to having so much money."

"Oh my gosh, I think I'm hyperventilating." Ivy's breaths were coming out in shallow, rapid bursts.

"Ivy, honey, look at me." He kept glancing at her and back at the road. "It'll all be okay. You're going to get used to it. I'm still me and you're still you. Who knows, you might find a hidden shopping diva inside of you that has never had a chance to escape."

Ivy snorted and Eli relaxed. The sound reassured him she was calming back down. "I doubt it. I wouldn't know what to do if you gave me any spending money."

Eli brought her hand to his lips. "Well, Vegas is the perfect place to figure that out."

"We're really going to elope?"

"Absolutely." Eli grinned. Eli felt freer than he ever had before. For the first time in his life, he had thrown off the barriers he held so strictly to and taken a plunge over the edge.

EPILOGUE

Nelson clapped and tilted his head in a sarcastic manner as Eli and Ivy walked down the steps of the plane.

Hayden stood close by, his arms folded over his chest and a small smile on his face.

"Were you two really in such a hurry that you had to leave us high and dry in a town two hours from home?"

Eli grinned. "Looks like you made it all right."

Nelson snorted. "No thanks to you."

"Sorry, Nellie," Ivy said with a smile. "We decided we had waited long enough."

"Nellie?" Hayden burst into laughter and Nelson glared.

Eli chuckled. "Oh, yeah," he rubbed the stubble on his chin, "I never did get around to telling him about that nickname."

Nelson rolled his eyes. "It's a good thing I like you so much, Little Sister, or I'd have to do something about it."

Ivy's smile was wide, and she leaned in, wrapping her arms around Eli. "Little Sister, I like the sound of that."

"Me too, Fairy-Girl," Nelson grinned.

Ivy rolled her eyes and huffed.

"Welcome to the family." Hayden came forward and held out his hand.

Ivy looked at his hand, up at his face, then walked forward and gave him a hug.

Hayden held his arms out and looked at Eli with a panicked expression.

Eli shrugged and smiled.

"Thank you, Hayden," Ivy said softly as she backed up into Eli's arms.

"Oh, let me see," Nelson teased in a high pitch voice as he reached for Ivy's ring finger.

Ivy's cheeks turned bright red as Nelson whistled over the size of the rock on her finger. She looked over her shoulder. "I told you it was too big," she scolded Eli.

"Absolutely not," Eli kissed the top of her head. "It's perfect."

Ivy had picked out a simple band with a solitaire on it but Eli had turned down his nose at it. Once he figured out what style she liked, he and the thrilled jeweler found a diamond several sizes larger than Ivy was willing to ask for herself.

"I told you," Eli whispered in her ear, "there are perks to being a billionaire."

"Billionaire or not, I'm just grateful you're mine," Ivy whispered back.

"Me too," Eli closed the gap between them and sealed the deal a kiss.

THE END

Did You Enjoy This Book?

Thank you so much for reading my story! I hope you enjoyed it. The best way to show your appreciation to an author is through a review! Even if it's only a couple of words, reviews are so appreciated and really help an author get their name heard.

You can find more of my books at lauraannbooks.com

Made in the USA
Middletown, DE
27 January 2023

23339255R00116